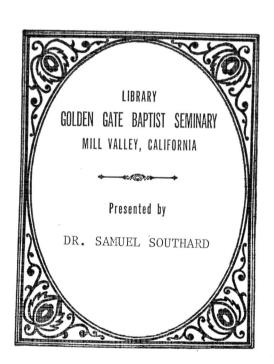

Families with Purpose

The William M. Pinsons (Left to right): Bobbie, Meredith, Allison, Bill

ABOUT THE AUTHOR

Dr. William M. Pinson, Jr. is president of Golden Gate Baptist Theological Seminary, Mill Valley, California. Prior to coming to Golden Gate Dr. Pinson served as pastor of First Baptist Church, Wichita Falls, Texas and as Professor of Christian Ethics at Southwestern Baptist Theological Seminary in Fort Worth. Dr. Pinson is a recipient of the Christian Life Commission's Distinguished Service Award. Preaching about family life has been a part of Dr. Pinson's ministry from its beginning. As a pastor Dr. Pinson developed a comprehensive program of ministering to families. As a seminary president one of his highest priorities is the establishment of a family enrichment program to strengthen the families of students, faculty and staff.

Families With Purpose

William M. Pinson, Jr.

BROADMAN PRESS
Nashville, Tennessee

To

the family of faith known as

The First Baptist Church, Wichita Falls, Texas

who made our family part of her family

and

whom we will love and be part of for the rest of life

© Copyright 1978 • Broadman Press.
All rights reserved.
4256–28
ISBN: 0-8054-5628-7

Dewey Decimal Classification: 301.52
Subject headings: FAMILY // MARRIAGE
Library of Congress Catalog Card Number: 78–057932
Printed in the United States of America

Foreword

The family is God's idea. He created the family to provide personal and spiritual enrichment for human beings. The family is the most durable institution of all time. It has survived the crises of history and moved society from era to era. But the family has always had its troubles, and it often falls short of God's ideal. The modern family is coming apart at the alarming rate of over one million divorces a year. Thus, ministers are now turning their approach to ministry toward family enrichment. That is why this book is so timely and relevant.

Families with Purpose is a preachable series of sermons that deal with family life at the major stages of development. Issues that create family stress are dealt with positively and practically.

These sermons are built on a solid biblical base, a sound theology, and daily experiences of healthy family living. The insights from the Scriptures and illustrations from daily life bring vitality and excitement to each sermon. The sermons were first preached by Dr. William Pinson when he was pastor of the First Baptist Church, Wichita Falls, Texas, and then delivered at the National Family Enrichment Conference at Glorieta Baptist Conference Center, where he was the guest preacher. They will meet a real need of the minister in preaching and teaching family enrichment.

Families with Purpose is a valuable resource which will assist the minister in fulfilling his commitment to enrich the family life in his congregation through his preaching.

JOSEPH W. HINKLE, SECRETARY

Family Ministry Department
Sunday School Board of the Southern
Baptist Convention

Preface

Preaching about family life has been a part of my ministry from its beginning. As a seminary professor I thoroughly enjoyed teaching God's truth about family life. As a pastor it was a joy to help develop a special family enrichment program at the First Baptist Church in Wichita Falls, Texas. As a seminary president, one of my highest priorities is the establishment of a family enrichment program to strengthen the families of students, faculty, and staff and to prepare church leaders for ministering effectively to families.

These sermons are just that—sermons. They are not essays about family; nor are they speeches. Each one is rooted in the Bible and is an effort to proclaim God's Word concerning family life. Most were preached at the First Baptist Church in Wichita Falls. They grew out of the context of ministry.

These sermons were selected from a large number of sermons primarily on the basis of providing a diversity. The first group deals with family life on the basis of the family cycle, from marriage to the birth of children to the middle years to old age. The second group relates family life to special days and emphases—holidays, Mother's Day, Father's Day, Christian discipleship. Not all family-related topics are included, of course. The scope of the book is too limited for that. The chapter on how to conduct family ministry in a local church shows how many topics could be included. The collection of Scriptures demonstrates the large amount of material in the Bible on family life.

Many people have contributed to the development of this

book. My family has been the primary contributor. Being a part of a Christian family provides the best kind of insight and experience out of which to speak and to write. I am deeply grateful to Bobbie, Meredith, and Allison for their contribution and ministry to me and through me.

The family of faith at First Baptist Church, Wichita Falls, Texas, contributed a great deal. They provided insight on what a church family ought to be, responded to leadership suggestions about the development of a family enrichment program, and through openness and honesty gave me insight into how the gospel works in the lives of families.

The seminary family at Golden Gate Baptist Theological Seminary has contributed. In the interchange of family, staff, and students, I continue to learn about the ways God works in family life. A number of faculty and staff members have made suggestions about which sermons to include and how to clarify points being made. Within the seminary family Wanda Phifer did a marvelous job of typing the transcripts and developing the final copy. Working with her in a cooperative venture were Janis McCracken, Jan Franklin, and Bonnie Chappell. Myra Ottewell also provided essential help.

Parents, in-laws, relatives, and various other members of our extended family have provided a firm ground for observation and learning. I am grateful to each one of them.

Finally, this book has been made possible by the splendid editorial staff of Broadman Press, the outstanding leadership of the Family Ministry Department of the Sunday School Board, and by the Family Life Task Force of the Baptist General Convention of Texas, under the executive leadership of Dr. James H. Landes. I am deeply grateful to be a part of a denominational family that majors on family.

WILLIAM M. PINSON, JR.

Mill Valley, California
May 1978

Contents

Part 1: The Family Cycle 11

   1. A Union with Purpose 11
   2. Sex Is for Marriage 23
   3. Is There Life After Birth? 34
   4. The Three Stages of Man 48
   5. Midcourse Correction 58
   6. When You Will Be Old 66
   7. Becoming Single 75

Part 2: Special Days and Special Times 83

   8. Giving Birth to a Baby Doesn't Make You a
      Mother 83
      (Mother's Day)
   9. When Fathers Fail 92
      (Father's Day)
  10. Christian Discipleship and Family Life 101
      (Revival)
  11. Aging: A Christian Response 110
      (Senior Adult Day)
  12. Handling the Holidays 120
      (Christmas)

How to Conduct Family Ministry in a Local Church   129
Scripture and Family   145
Index of Scripture References   161
Subject Index   164

Part 1: The Family Cycle

1

A Union with Purpose

And the Lord God said, It is not good that the man should be alone; I will make him an help meet for him.

And out of the ground the Lord God formed every beast of the field, and every fowl of the air; and brought them unto Adam to see what he would call them: and whatsoever Adam called every living creature, that was the name thereof.

And Adam gave names to all cattle, and to the fowl of the air, and to every beast of the field; but for Adam there was not found an help meet for him.

And the Lord God caused a deep sleep to fall upon Adam, and he slept: and he took one of his ribs, and closed up the flesh instead thereof;

And the rib, which the Lord God had taken from man, made he a woman, and brought her unto the man.

And Adam said, This is now bone of my bones, and flesh of my flesh: she shall be called Woman, because she was taken out of Man.

Therefore shall a man leave his father and his mother, and shall cleave unto his wife: and they shall be one flesh (Gen. 2:18–24).

"We want to get married."

"Why?"

"Well," (giggle), "I don't know. Because we love each other, I guess."

"What does that have to do with getting married? You love a lot of people, don't you?"

"Yes. But this is different."

"How is it different? What makes you think you ought to be married?"

And so the conversation goes between a couple and a pastor talking about marriage. An alarming number of people don't seem to know what marriage really is—not from a biblical point of view, anyway. Nor do they know what the real basis of marriage is. Myths about marriage rather than God's Word seem to dominate attitudes about marriage.

You've heard the myths expressed, haven't you? "When you fall in love, you ought to get married." "If two people love each other, everything will work out." "Happy homes just happen when two people who are right for one another get married." Or maybe you're familiar with some of the less romantic myths: "A trial marriage will show whether two people are really meant to be married and will save the mess of divorce." "Marriage should be open-ended, based on a mutual relationship which can be terminated by either party so no one will get hurt." "Marriage is an out-of-date institution and should be replaced by meaningful relationships based on mutual love between two consenting adults."

Marriage should not be based on such myths but on truth. That truth is the Bible's teaching on marriage and family. God has revealed through the Bible that marriage is essentially a union of a man and woman in the will of God for the purpose of companionship, sexual relationship, and the birth and nurture of children. It is a union with purpose.

A good marriage, like any other good relationship in life, takes planning and work. Most people seem to understand this principle in other areas but ignore it in marriage and family. We spend a great deal of time planning and preparing for a vocation, for example. Many people take years preparing for a particular vocation; they go to trade school, apprentice, attend college, or study in a professional school. On the other hand, many people don't spend any time at all getting ready to be married. You must prepare for years to be licensed or certified to practice law or medicine, teach school, or work as an architect. But no training is required to get a marriage license. It's easier to get a marriage license than to get a driver's license.

Lack of preparation for marriage frequently leads to lack of effort within a marriage to make it what God intended. Some people spend more time polishing up their golf game than they do trying to have a better family. Others exert more energy to make money than they do to have a Christian home. Our priorities get twisted; and, as a result, our families frequently suffer.

A happy home doesn't just happen. You have to work at it. It takes effort. No one thinks that a winning football team just happens. Everyone understands that it takes planning and work to have one. A choir doesn't produce a great sound by just getting together and singing. It takes work and discipline. A business can't succeed without work. A church won't grow without effort. Yet most of us harbor the hope that our families will be able to make it all right without any extra effort; we practice what we believe, and families drift—frequently to catastrophe.

But it is not enough to work hard. You also have to know what you are doing. Some people work very hard to have a winning football team but they don't win. Some people work very hard to make a success of their business but they go bankrupt. Some people work diligently to make their church grow but it still doesn't grow. Why? Something more than work is necessary; you have to know what you are doing. Hard work plus the right formula can equal success.

I am grateful to be a Christian for many reasons. One of them is that in my family life I have the Bible to guide me and the indwelling Lord to give me the help I need as I work to follow the Bible's guidelines. With those resources I have what I need to develop a whole and happy family life. Let's see what the Word of God teaches about marriage and family.

The Bible says in Genesis 2:24 and Matthew 19:4-6 that a marriage is basically a union: "Therefore shall a man leave his father and his mother, and shall cleave unto his wife: and they shall be one flesh." One plus one in God's marital mathematics equals one. The word *joined* pictures two items being glued or welded together so that each maintains an identity while becoming part of something new, not two liquids poured together so that each loses its identity in the new mixture. That's important. Marriage does not make two persons new; marriage relates two persons in a new way.

This union is very special. It is not merely a human relationship that can be broken at the whims of the parties involved. It is a sacred union. It is not like a secular contract that can be broken by a skilled attorney who knows how to use the law to terminate a relationship. Rather, it is a sacred union, a divinely ordained union. God joins the two together, the Bible says, in his will for a purpose.

The basis of marriage ought to be the will of God for two people, not the love of two people for each other. Most persons fall in love more than once during life. When I was a seminary professor I polled students in class to see how many of them had been in love at least three times. In most classes 80 percent of them indicated they had. Many confessed that even after they had been married they felt the "love" emotion—that strange sensation in the pit of the stomach accompanied by palpitating pulse, loss of appetite, and weakness in the knees— about someone other than their mate. They had not had an affair or been sexually unfaithful; they simply had that "in love" feeling. When a spouse dies, the survivor often forms another marriage that is just as happy and wonderful as the one before. God has given us great capacity to love.

Since you cannot marry everyone with whom you fall in love, there must be something else than just "I love you" on which to base a marriage. Yet many plunge into marriage with no more than that.

Quite often in the spring I'll notice a girl showing off a rock on her finger. I say to her, "Oh, I see you are engaged!" To myself, knowing the boy, I say, "Oh, no!" Later, in private, I ask, "Why are you marrying him?" "Oh, I love him," she sighs. "Yes, I can understand that, but why are you marrying him? It is not enough that you love him. Do you believe it is God's will that you marry him?"

Of course, you should not marry somone you don't love. You ought to love the person you marry, but you can't marry every person you love. Some other criterion for choice must be used—God's will. The best possible marriage can only be established when two people have a strong conviction that God's will is the basis of the marriage. This is a sacred union.

The Bible declares that marriage, in addition to being a sacred union, ought to be a lasting union. The Scripture makes it quite clear that divorce is at best failure. God intends marriages to last a lifetime. Jesus said concerning marriage, "What therefore God hath joined together, let not man put asunder" (Matt. 19:6). When reminded that divorce was practiced, Jesus replied, "But from the beginning it was not so" (Matt. 19:8). God's plan from the start was for a marriage to last a lifetime. Those who have been through the hurt of divorce usually testify that lasting marriage is the best kind of marriage.

When divorce shatters a marriage, a church has a responsibility to minister to those who have been hurt by the divorce, whose lives have been torn apart. A church should relate to divorced persons in a healing and redemptive way. After all, divorce is not the unpardonable sin. All of us have fallen short of the will of God in some ways. Each of us is a living testimony that God can forgive, God can restore, and life can be renewed. There is hope in Jesus Christ for the divorced person. This truth does not undermine the fact that marriage is made to last and that anyone who ignores the lasting feature of the marriage union will suffer.

The Bible also indicates that this union is to be an exclusive one. Jesus said, "For this cause shall a man leave father and mother, and shall cleave to his wife" (Matt. 19:15). Paul wrote, "Let every man have his own wife, and let every woman have her own husband" (1 Cor. 7:2). Marriage excludes sexual intercourse with anyone other than one's spouse. Adultery is clearly wrong. Yet some marriage counselors recommend an affair as a help for a sick marriage. Their line of reasoning is something like this: "If your marriage has gone stale, go out and have a good fling. It will add life to your marriage." But sexual exclusiveness is part of what marriage is. How can taking away part of the essence of a union make it stronger? The wages of sin is death, and adultery can do nothing but deal death to marriage. "Thou shalt not commit adultery" is part of God's law for us, given to us because he loves us and wants to guide us to life at its very best.

There is another kind of exclusiveness in marriage. The Bible says, "Therefore shall a man leave his father and his mother, and shall cleave unto his wife" (Gen. 2:24). This exclusiveness is sometimes difficult for Christians. They are not going to commit adultery, but to leave father and mother—and for father and mother to let go of them—is not easy. One Sunday night, at the beginning of a week's revival, as I was meeting the church members, a man came by, shook my hand limply, and stumbled out the door like a man in shock. He attended every night that week, and every night he looked closer to death than the night before—until Friday. Friday night he looked a little better, and by Sunday he had a sparkle in his eye. He came by after the closing service Sunday night and said, "I guess you have wondered about me." I answered, "Well, I must admit I've been a bit curious."

He explained, "The Saturday night before this revival began my baby daughter got married. We had done everything together. We had gone fishing together, cheered at ball games together. We'd had fun together. We'd often talk together for hours. And then she got married. I thought, *How could she do this to me?* With a sigh he continued, "They didn't even invite me on the honeymoon. I was hurt. All week I was mad, thinking they would call or check in. But I didn't hear anything. By Wednesday night I was unable to sleep. Suddenly Scriptures began to rumble through my mind, including the passage 'Forsaking father and mother and cleaving unto each other.' I realized that this was the way God intended it to be—for her to leave me and be joined to her husband.

I realized that as hard as it was for me, unless I somehow could let her go, I would violate God's will for her, for me, and for that marriage. So I began to pray for God to give me the strength to let her go. I have that victory."

I was happy. This marriage, which could have been doomed, now had a chance to succeed because of a change in the father's attitude. Exclusiveness means leaving father and mother, letting go of children so that they can form the union which God intends. In a marriage a new primary loyalty ought to be established between husband and wife, forsaking all others.

What is the purpose of marriage? The Bible teaches that this union has three purposes. The first purpose is companionship; God puts husband and wife together to be companions (Gen. 2:20–23). The second is sexual fulfillment. The Bible insists (1 Cor. 7:2–6) that sexual intimacy is part of marriage, that sex in marriage is not defiling (Heb. 13:4), that the marriage partners have a responsibility to meet the sexual needs of each other (1 Cor. 7). The third purpose is procreation (Gen. 1:28)—the bearing and rearing of children. It is not enough to conceive and give birth to children. Parents have a responsibility to care for their children's physical needs (1 Tim. 5:8), to teach them God's Word (Deut. 6:6–7), to train them (Prov. 22:6), to discipline and guide them (Eph. 6:4), and to provide them a good example (2 Tim. 1:5).

All of the purposes are bound up in the companionship concept. For example, sexual relations should grow out of and contribute to companionship, that special close feeling husband and wife ought to have for each other. If sex is merely an act or performance, it won't make this contribution. And if each party is not sensitive to the sexual needs of the other, then sexual activity can damage the companionship relation instead of help it.

Further, children are related to the companionship dimension of marriage as well as the sexual. Through sexual relations conception occurs, but the healthy development of the child depends to a large degree on a healthy home environment. And that in turn depends on the proper relation of husband and wife. If they relate well to each other, they will likely relate well to their children.

If intimate companionship is not part of a marriage, God's purpose for the marriage won't be carried out; and the couple will miss the happiness God planned for them. How do you develop and keep this kind of relationship? It takes effort—planning, communication, being sensitive to each other, unselfishness. A couple needs to take time to share and dream together.

Unfortunately, many couples don't keep the lines of communication open. I don't know what you do at mealtime when you are out alone. Some people read a paper or book; others tinker with the silverware. I have developed a game I play. I call it "people watching." When I go into a restaurant I pick out a couple to observe. As I watch them I seek answers for such questions as: Are they married? If they are, do they like it? How long have they been married? What kind of marriage do they have?

I have seen countless couples come into a restaurant, sit down, fiddle with the silverware, place their order, sip their water, eat their food, wipe their mouth, leave the tip, pay the check, depart—without having said one word to each other! Have you ever known anyone like that? They likely drive home in the same sort of stony silence. When they get home, about all the words between them are probably absolute essentials such as "Did you put the cat out?" or "What time do you have to get up in the morning?" There is no real sharing of life. God indicates that in marriage two people become one so that they can share with each other life's most intimate thoughts and experiences.

The ingredients of companionship are several, each important. A well-known Christian marriage counselor told me, "We have discovered in our counseling clinic that if there are four ingredients of a good marriage present between a husband and a wife, that marriage is going pretty well. If they *talk* together, if they *play and laugh* together, if they *work* together, and if they *pray* together, they will likely stay together and like it." Check your marriage by this list the next time things aren't going well, and I think you'll find one of these missing. Keep in mind the togetherness aspects of these. It is talking *together*, not one person telling the other something all the time—two people talking things over, remembering the past, planning the future, participating in the present. It is laughing *together*, playing *together*, recreating *together*. It is doing creative work *together* so that there is something about which you can say, "This is ours; we did it together." It is praying *together*, sharing worship and experiences with God.

Third, the Bible indicates that a family—this union established by God for a purpose—is to relate to one another in specific ways. Between husband and wife the Bible emphasizes love, fidelity, respect, and consideration for each other's needs (Titus 2:3–5; 1 Pet. 3:1–2,7). Read Ephesians 5:21–33 and 1 Corinthians 7:1–5 for extensive biblical guidelines on husband-wife relations. Between parents and children the key words for the children are obedience and honor (Eph 6:1–4); and for the parents they are love, discipline, nurture, provision, religious instruction.

The key word is love—parents for children, children for parents, husbands for wives, wives for husbands. Love is expressed by touch, words, attitude, and actions. The facets of love are displayed in the famous 1 Corinthians 13 passage. Use it as a checklist for your family's love life. Love sometimes can be best felt in the little things, in the courtesies of life. It is expressed through appreciation and thoughtfulness that lubricates the wheels of marriage, keeping down the heat which develops from the friction of daily life. It's the "Thank you, that was a wonderful meal!" instead of a burp and a silent exit to read the paper. It's the "Wow, you look great today." It's weeding out temper, anger, selfishness, greed, and the kinds of things that ruin relationships. It's eliminating carping criticism, the cruel put-down.

Many families dig at one another frequently; some parents

nag children almost constantly. In Ephesians Paul warned parents not to treat children in such a way that they provoked them to wrath. Have you ever heard parents say, "Why can't you be smart like your brother?" or "Why are you so clumsy? You can't walk through a room without knocking something over. If there is a snag in the carpet you'll fall over it." Or "Well, I see you have done your usual lousy job in your grades." Such negative, petty remarks sometimes pass between husband and wife: "You're a little pouchy there, aren't you?" "Why can't you keep the house as clean as your mother keeps hers?" "Another year without a promotion, huh?" Family members are not to use one another as a vent for their own anger and frustration but to relate to each other as Christ did to us—in love, with sacrifice and compassion. That makes family life wonderful.

Finally, the Bible has a great deal to say about how a family—this union with purpose—is to function. Basically, it is to function much as a church functions. The New Testament contains the phrase "the church in his house" (Col. 4:15). It probably relates to the fact that in the first century the Christians didn't have houses of worship as we do and people met in homes. But it also implies that every home needs to be like a church; in every house where Christians live there is to be a kind of church. Churches exist for many things. They exist for evangelism. They exist for ministry. They exist for Christian education. They exist for worship. A family is to do all of these. To the degree that a family does them all, it is strong in Christ.

Check your home to find out how the church in your house is doing. Is evangelism thriving there as members of your family are led to Christ as Lord and Savior, as you reach out to friends and neighbors with the gospel? Is ministry in Christ's name a function of your family—visiting the sick, caring for the aged, feeding the hungry, righting the wrongs in society? Is Christian education a part of every day through conversation, Bible study, and sharing?

And how about worship as a family? One of the important things the church in your house can do is make worship of the living God a celebration, a happy experience. This is important because some children grow up with a negative idea about God. They think God means trouble. In their homes the only time God is mentioned is when there is trouble: "Daddy lost his job; let's pray he'll get another." "Mother has to have an operation; let's pray she'll get well soon." "Grandmother died because God took her to be with him." Sunday morning for many churchgoing families is a weekly catastrophe, the worst time of the week. Sometimes more religion is lost by a family getting to the church house than is regained after they arrive.

You know the scene. Little children who other mornings sleep late get up bright and early on Sunday. Everybody else wants to sleep. The tots pad around the house having a great time; Mother gets up, thinks she'll do a good thing, and dresses them early. Then the parents get the teenagers up—grapefruit juice, ice down the pajamas, anything to get them awake in the morning. By the time the teenagers are dressed the little ones have made mud pies on their tummies or are washing toothbrushes in the toilets. So they have to be dressed all over again. Then Daddy gets on the horn—honk! honk!—and yells, "Come on. We're going to be late again."

Finally the family is on the way to worship God—grumpy, sullen, angry. They get to church and everybody goes to Sunday School, where they regain some composure. Then they go to worship. Soon the little ones get restless. Mamma takes out her survival kit—paper, pencils, crayons, and so forth. The children draw happily for a while until someone sitting nearby says, "Shhh!" Mother pinches the children, warns them to be quiet, and puts up the survival kit. Soon the youngsters go to sleep. The impression begins to form that God is bad news. The child thinks, *Whenever God is in the picture we fuss. When we worship God, I get bored, pinched, and sleepy.*

Not all families are like this, of course, but many are. To counteract this negative input the family needs to celebrate the presence of the living God. Day-by-day activities should become a kind of prayer meeting. When you have a birthday party and ice cream is still dripping off the wall and clutter is all over the floor, it's time to kneel and thank God for the joy of friendship. When the first flower pushes its way up through the soil in the spring, it's time for a prayer meeting in the backyard, thanking God for the beauty of nature. When you come home safe from a trip and you've had great fun, it's time to thank God for fun and family fellowship. When you've just got a new puppy and everyone is excited, thank God for the gift of wiggly, warm, cuddly life. Make worship a celebration experience.

Certainly there is a time for discipline. People must learn to sit through things they don't enjoy. But how awful if a family associates God only with discord, discipline, dullness, and disaster. God loves us in Jesus Christ with the promise of life abundant. A family should allow the living Lord to dwell with them. We should let him become so much a part of us that we celebrate with joy his presence daily. Then family will become, day by day, a living experience of people together in love because they have been brought together by our Lord.

"But," you say, "I can never live up to this standard for a family." You are correct. None of us is able to do this on his own. It takes help from many sources but primarily from the One who created the family. No one can have a Christian home without being a Christian. You become a Christian through turning away from a "do-it-myself" attitude to one of repentance and faith in Jesus Christ. Then he comes to dwell with you to help you. He gives the Holy Spirit to empower you.

Wouldn't you like to have a real Christian home? Wouldn't you like to have the kind of family in which God is very real and Jesus Christ is Lord and love reigns supreme? Wouldn't you like to be part of a family with purpose—God's purpose? You can, and the beginning can be right now.

2

Sex Is for Marriage

Thou shalt not commit adultery (Ex. 20:14).

Ye have heard that it was said by them of old time, Thou shalt not commit adultery: But I say unto you, That whosoever looketh on a woman to lust after her hath committed adultery with her already in his heart (Matt. 5:27–28).

Adultery isn't confined to television soap operas, pulp novels, "R" rated movies, or families who don't go to church. I don't need the findings of surveys on the sexual practices of Americans to know that adultery is more common than we'd like to admit. Pastors and counselors frequently deal with persons whose marriages and lives have been shattered by adultery. Rather than pretend such is not the case, it is better to face the unpleasant facts and do what we can to help people who are involved in this terribly destructive sin. God takes a frank approach in his word. "Thou shall not commit adultery" is one of the Ten Commandments.

God gave us the Ten Commandments not because he's some sort of spoilsport who doesn't want anyone to have fun, but because he wants us to have life at its best. Because he made us and knows how we are to function, he's given us a kind of owner's manual to follow so that we can have the smoothest running life possible—or as Jesus put it, that we might "have life, and . . . have it more abundantly" (John 10:10). Although the commandments sometimes are expressed in negative ways—"thou shalt not"—behind each negative commandment is a positive purpose for life.

These commandments are given for a community, not just for individuals. They are the ingredients necessary for a society to exist. If these commandments are not followed there cannot be true community. In these laws for life we're not dealing with peripheral matters but with the heart of what it means to be human, with what God wills for each of us as well as for all of us in community. None of these commandments, therefore, is superfluous. None of them is to be considered for a part of the community and not for all. As David discovered, not even kings were exempt.

In the Old Testament one of the key commandments is "Thou shalt not commit adultery." The New Testament records Jesus' comment on the commandment, "Ye have heard that it was said by them of old time, Thou shalt not commit adultery. But I say unto you, That whosoever looketh on a woman to lust after her hath committed adultery with her already in his heart. And if thy right eye offend thee, pluck it out, and cast it from thee; for it is profitable for thee that one of thy members should perish, and not that thy whole body should be cast into hell. And if thy right hand offend thee, cut it off and cast it from thee; for it is profitable for thee that one of thy members should perish, and not that thy whole body should be cast into hell" (Matt. 5:27–30). The commandment "Thou shalt not commit adultery" has one specific and clear meaning: People who are married are not to have sexual relationships with any person other than the one to whom they are married.

The Bible deals with many different aspects of human sexuality. God doesn't blush when he speaks to us about sex. The Bible is forthright in discussing this ingredient of human life. According to the Bible, sexual intercourse is to be limited to heterosexual relations between a male and a female who are married to each other. God's Word contains teachings about incest, bestiality, homosexuality, and fornication. But this particular commandment deals with adultery. Jesus expanded on the commandment and indicated that adultery relates not only to an action but also to an attitude. Jesus taught that attitude leads to action—that as a person thinks in his heart, so he becomes. Adultery is not something that just happens; it is part of a process. It begins with a look that evokes lust which leads to immoral action. Some have interpreted Jesus' statement to mean that any look at a person who is a member of the complementary sex is wrong. That's not what he said. Jesus spoke of a lingering look upon a woman to the extent that a man's sexual desire was kindled and nurtured.

A person who looks with lust, who imagines sexual intercourse with a person other than a mate, has already committed a kind of adultery; a promise of fidelity has already been undermined. But it doesn't mean that what is done within one's attitude or imagination is the same as what is done in action. The persons in the marriage are affected, but the third party is not. If attitude leads to action, then the third party would be involved. Jesus was speaking to people who believed that by keeping the details of the law, they would please God. He wanted them to understand that attitude is important too, that attitude affects action, that God looks on the heart. Jesus warned to guard carefully how we look on others and to avoid lustful attitudes which can lead to activity contrary to God's directions for abundant life. Christian discipline includes the eyes and thoughts.

The other side of the coin is that people should not deliberately try to incite adulterous attitudes. Pornography, obscene movies, and television programs that excite adulterous attitudes are contrary to what the Bible teaches about sexuality. The way a person dresses or fails to dress, the way an individual walks, stance and posture designed primarily to gain attention and stimulate sexual desire—any activity intended to attract a lustful look is out of bounds for the follower of Jesus Christ. The people of God have a responsibility not to excite lustful attitudes in others which can result in adulterous activity.

Why does the Bible take adultery so seriously? Our culture doesn't. Many jokes, plays, dramas, TV programs, movies, books, novels, and short stories make light of adultery. They communicate that it really doesn't make much difference whether a person commits adultery or not, that adultery is just "one of those things" and we ought not get too upset about it. Why does God take such a directly contrary stand? Why is the Bible's view in regard to adultery so different from our modern culture's?

The Bible does take adultery very seriously, you know. Adultery was punishable by death according to the Old Testament Law. Adultery is used in the Bible as a symbol of the unfaithfulness of the Hebrews to God. The account in the book of Hosea about an adulterous wife who broke the heart of her husband is seen as a kind of parable of how we break the heart of God when we fail to be faithful to him. If the Bible takes adultery seriously, we must not treat it lightly.

But why is adultery wrong? The Bible teaches that adultery undercuts a very important aspect of our humanity—sexuality and the responsible use of it. Some people insist that Christians have created all the sexual problems in our world by following an antisex approach to life, that guilt and abnormal behavior are the result of Christian standards for sex. The fact is that every society throughout history has had certain requirements and restrictions regarding sexuality. It's too powerful a drive, too important a part of human life, not to have some controls. The Puritans didn't originate sexual restriction; neither did the Victorians. Restrictions on sexual activity have always been part of human history. They are part of the Bible's guide for human conduct, too.

God is not antisexual. In fact, he created sex. God makes it clear in his word that we were created as sexual beings: "Male and female created he them. And God blessed them, and God said unto them, Be fruitful and multiply" (Gen. 1:27–28). The Bible indicates that sexual relations in marriage are in the will of God; sexuality correctly expressed is good

(Heb. 13:4). God gives explicit instructions that husband and wife are to provide each other sexual satisfaction (1 Cor. 7:1–5).

Sex in marriage can be wrong if it doesn't provide this satisfaction. Being married does not give a person a license to do anything he or she pleases regarding sex. Sex within marriage is to strengthen the marriage, not weaken it—is to be constructive, not destructive. Cruel, abusive, manipulative, dehumanizing sexual expressions have no place in marriage. Being insensitive and unresponsive to a spouse's sexual needs is not only irresponsible but is also contrary to the word of God.

The Bible clearly reveals that God is not against sex responsibly expressed. However, God knows what he's created and that it ought to function for our good and not our harm. Many things that he created for our good have been misused. Like any other good but powerful drive, sex can be abused and turned into something destructive.

Among the drives and instincts with which God equipped us, sex is not the only one subject to abuse. A drive even more basic than sex is hunger. When a person misuses the hunger drive, he is living in order to eat instead of eating in order to live. He consumes more than the body needs, and the pounds begin to show in bulges of fat. Most who are overweight are guilty of abusing one of the basic drives God built into human life. The desire for accumulating, building, and constructing is another basic drive. If we didn't have it, we would be poor beasts indeed. It's what leads us to construct beautiful buildings and accumulate possessions needed for the ongoing of life. But it too can be abused. Greed and pride cause us to exploit one another. We collect stuff to the point that it's difficult to move about in our homes. Instead of possessing things, things begin to possess us. We have abused what God gave us for good.

And so with sexuality—used rightly it's good, but used wrongly it's destructive. In popular romantic jargon sex is often compared to fire: "You light my fire" means a person is sexually attractive. Fire can be good—warming a cold house, cooking food, lighting a dark room—if it is used properly and kept under control. Allowed to rage out of control, it will burn down the house, cremate the food, and destroy the people in the room. So it is with sex. It can be constructive or destructive depending on how it's used. Yet there are people who want to treat sex casually; they say we ought to do what comes naturally. They insist that Christians have tried to enforce unnatural standards of conduct in human life. Fire, left uncontrolled to do what is natural, will destroy a forest. Sex, left uncontrolled to do what is natural, will destroy a life.

We need some sort of standard by which to guide human life; that is what the Bible provides. The Bible teaches that sexual intercourse is to be between a man and a woman married to each other; that kind of sexual expression has constructive potential for human life and society. On the negative side the Bible declares, "Thou shalt not commit adultery."

But why is sexual intercourse right only within marriage? One answer is found in the book of Genesis, in the story of creation. Genesis records that *'Adam* needed a companion. The animals did not fill this need, and God created woman. The Hebrew word *'ish* is used for the male and *'ishah* for the female. Each is incomplete without the other, according to the creation story. Each yearns for the other; there's a tug pulling them together. One aspect of that tug is sexual desire, a yearning to be close to each other and to merge their bodies together. "They shall be one flesh," the Bible states (Gen. 2:24).

Sexuality, therefore, is an expression of what God intended from the very beginning, an harmonious relating of male and female, of *'ish* and *'ishah*. A by-product of sexual union is procreation; but the main purpose is unification, two lives blended together by God. That can only take place within marriage. Casual sex is not a violation of a minor moral code but of what we were created to be. God created *one* man and *one* woman together to be the model for sexual relations; sex with multiple partners is contrary to his intent and our welfare. Sexual intercourse is the symbol of two persons becoming one flesh committed to each other for life; sexual intercourse apart from that commitment is a mockery of what it means to be human.

Marriage is leaving the security of mother and father, establishing a new primary loyalty, being joined to husband or wife as one flesh, caring for this new part of you as you care for yourself; adultery flies in the face of all the Bible teaches about the meaning, wonder, and purpose of marriage. Sexual intercourse outside of marriage is a violation of God's created order and will bring hurt to those involved.

Some want the only standard for sex to be pleasure. If it brings pleasure, it's all right, they say. Sex should bring pleasure; but if that is the only standard, we might as well be animals. There's more to sex than fun. An act of sexual intercourse should be an act of communion, not just of union, in which two people are brought together to share one of life's most intimate experiences. Sex in marriage is the only way sex is in harmony with our created nature; sex out of marriage results in disharmony, strife, and pain.

Sexuality is part of our being made in the image of God. The Bible says that "God created man in his own image, . . . male and female created he them" (Gen. 1:27). God chose to continue his act of creation through human procreation. We are acting as persons created in the image of God when we involve ourselves in responsible procreation. God creates; we procreate. God created the universe and all that is within it and gave us life. Then God appointed us as his servants on earth, his stewards of the world he'd created, and gave us the ability to procreate, to multiply life.

The setting for procreation is the family. Sex outside the marriage relationship violates the procreative aspect of our creation. God did not create the world and then abandon it. He continues to sustain and to care for his creation. To conceive and then irresponsibly abort or abandon a baby is contrary to what it means to be made in the image of God. Every act of sexual intercourse need not have conception as its goal; sex in marriage is primarily for unification, not procreation. Yet most acts of sexual intercourse have the potential for conception. A couple should be willing to support, nurture, and love a child conceived by them. Within a family, specifically a marriage, is where such care is best provided.

From the Bible it's clear why adultery is not to be taken lightly. It's not just a matter of someone having sex with a person outside of marriage. Whether it's a one-time event or a continuing affair, it is not simply a flippant moment in human history that doesn't amount to much. It amounts to a great deal, for it is the denial of what God created us to be. It makes mockery of what male-female relationships ought to be. It stands in the way of knowing abundant life. It robs us of the full benefit of being created in his image. It's serious indeed. That's why in an expression of love for us God said, "Thou shalt not commit adultery."

There are other reasons, less basic but important, why adultery is wrong. Adultery undermines family stability. You can't have a stable family if you have mothers and fathers—husbands and wives—who are involved in adultery. Although some insist that an affair is good for a marriage, there's no valid evidence that such behavior strengthens a marriage relationship. No, adultery undermines marriage. Since the essence of marriage is trust and fidelity, how can a violation of that trust through infidelity improve a relationship? It can't.

Adultery is wrong because it hurts people. There are always at least three persons involved in adultery, but usually there are dozens of people involved—children, grandchildren, aunts, uncles, communities, church members, friends. Adultery is not something you do in isolation. Adultery is an act against the community. It brings hurt to many. If you really love, if you really care, don't commit adultery. If you care for yourself, if you care for your mate, if you care for your children, if you care for society, don't commit adultery.

Some claim they commit adultery out of love, but adultery is not an act of love. It is a selfish, irresponsible act, the very opposite of love. Valid human love grows out of love for God, but how can one love God and violate his commandments? Love builds relationships; adultery destroys relationships. To excuse adultery on the basis of love is blind rationalization.

Another reason adultery is wrong is that it leads to other wrongs. The story of David and Bathsheba is a classic expression of human sinfulness; it demonstrates that adultery doesn't stop with adultery. David saw Bathsheba bathing and instead of turning away he looked and lusted. Lust was not stopped short but was allowed to grow until David committed adultery. Then he lied and murdered. He violated command after command of the God he professed to love and serve. Sin has a way of compounding itself. What starts out to be a simple affair turns into a complex tragedy.

Selfishness, lies, deceit, covetousness, false witness, and taking God's name in vain usually go along with adultery. Not infrequently it leads to violence, divorce, and even murder. It always hurts. Adultery is rejection, violation of trust, breaking of promises, seeking to satisfy self regardless of the cost to others. It is made up of the stuff that destroys not only families but civilizations. No wonder God warned, "Thou shalt not commit adultery." He loves us.

What's the remedy? The best preventive measures for adultery are a right relationship with God and other people, the belief that God's way is best, the inner strength that comes from the Spirit of God in us, an understanding that God's laws are given not to diminish but to increase the abundance of life. Adultery can be avoided by avoiding the conditions that contribute to adultery, such as lustful staring, being alone with a person who is sexually available, fantasizing about sexual activity with someone other than one's spouse.

A strong defense against adultery is a stable, warm, satisfying marriage. A Christian should utilize the power of God within to help resist temptation to commit adultery. The power that is within us as Christians is greater than the power that is in the world. Consistent worship, daily prayer, sensitivity to the Holy Spirit's direction and Bible meditation strengthens the Christian for times of temptation. Growing in Christian maturity is an excellent antidote to adultery.

Many adulterers make excuses, perhaps to ease their guilt. The excuses are feeble. Some say, "Adultery is all right because it's harmful to repress sexual desire." It's not harmful to repress our desires. The only way society can exist is to control desires. If I want to hit you in the mouth when I meet you on the street, should I give in to my feelings? No! Civilization cannot exist when people give way to their desires. Others say, "Adultery is good for you; it's liberating. And it often adds life to marriage." But how can it be good if it's a violation of what God has created us to be, of God's command and will?

Some say, "I'm just not getting enough sexual satisfaction at home, so I need to get it outside." The answer to that is to work with your mate for a better marriage and disciplined desire. Many claim, "I acted out of love; I love her (him)." But real love is more than sexual desire or even a yearning for companionship. Love doesn't hurt the one loved, but adultery is hurtful. Furthermore, love does not nullify God's will, marriage promises, or responsible living.

What should you do if you fall short of God's standards, if you commit adultery? You should do what you do when any other sin is involved—greed, theft, murder, or jealousy. You stop, repent, confess, seek God's forgiveness, and do what you can to mend the damage you have done. God is ready to forgive us and cleanse us from all unrighteousness if we come to him contrite, brokenhearted, wanting to change our ways, confessing, and believing that he will forgive us and help us. He can't take away all the hurt or undo the damage that's been done, but he can take away the guilt, forgive, and set you on a new course. That's the hope of the gospel. Through faith in Jesus Christ who loved us, died for us, and rose from the grave, there is new life. That's why the word about Jesus is good news. Nothing is beyond his forgiveness—even adultery.

3

Is There Life After Birth?

Ask, and it shall be given you; seek, and ye shall find; knock, and it shall be opened unto you . . .

For every one that seeketh findeth; and to him that knocketh it shall be opened.

Or what man is there of you, whom if his son ask bread, will give him a stone?

Or if he ask a fish, will he give him a serpent?

If ye then, being evil, know how to give good gifts unto your children, how much more shall your Father which is in heaven give good things to them that ask him? (Matt.7:7–11).

Is there life after birth? Maybe. Many babies who are born never really live; they grow up only existing. Parents are primarily responsible for seeing that there is life after birth. Some parents do their job very well; others fail miserably. I've never known anyone who was intentionally a bad parent. Parents fall short not because of malice toward their children but usually because of ignorance of what good parenting really is.

Parenting must be done primarily while the children are young and at home. It involves a relatively small part of an adult's life; but when the opportunity is gone, it's gone forever. You can major on such things as hobbies, entertainment, profession, and investments at almost any time, but you can major on being a parent during only a small slice of life.

The earliest years are the most important. By the time a child reaches the age of five or six, most of his personality and character are already established. Life after birth is closely related to the first years. What a parent does he must do quickly, for soon it is too late to parent. But what does good parenting involve?

A few years ago I was asked to preach a sermon on family life for the annual meeting of a Baptist state convention. I enlisted several people to aid me in researching for it. We divided the research into three sections. One group compiled what the Bible taught about family. Another group surveyed what the best Christian sociologists and psychiatrists were saying about parent-child relationships. And I interviewed people who seemed to have done a first-rate job of raising children, people whose children were already grown and out in the world living for God and serving others. When we compared the research findings we discovered seven common factors necessary in a family for the proper development of a child.

There is no magic in these seven ingredients. Family life is too complex to reduce to an oversimplified formula. But these seven are important—biblically, psychologically, sociologically, and experientially. They seem to be part of God's plan for parent-child relations. When we omit one or more, things begin to go wrong. If they are present, things go well and a child develops according to the way God planned, for God has a plan for every life. If parents aren't living in the will of the Father and walking according to his love, then their children suffer a severe disadvantage and may never know real life.

The first ingredient necessary for life after birth is love. Some may say, "There's no need to emphasize love; all parents love their children." Unfortunately, some don't. And many of us love our children imperfectly. Love lets a child know he's special, that he's regarded as a gift from God and not a burden. When parents enjoy a child and bathe him in love, that child thrives. Without love, life shrivels.

A college student with whom I was talking expressed great hostility toward God. She described what she planned to do when she returned to her campus—drink, sleep around, make the drug scene—to show God what she thought of him. As I talked with her, I found that she really wasn't mad at God; she was angry with her father. He was a rigid, cold, aloof man. They never played or laughed together. He displayed no affection for her but always gave rules to her. He nagged, griped, and found fault with her. She needed desperately, as all of us do, to be loved. But her father rejected her. And the life that was to be never developed in her; she died bit by bit, consumed by hurt and anger. There was no life after birth.

Love is expressed in at least four different ways, each of them important. It's expressed by touch—hugs, kisses, pats—all the physical ways that one communicates "I love you." A friend of mine who was in charge of a home for unwed mothers discovered that newborn infants who were just kept in their beds and fed didn't develop physically, mentally, and emotionally as rapidly as those who were picked up, talked to, carried about, and rocked. So he instructed the persons working in the nursery to pick up all the babies, carry them around, and talk to them. Providing them with the feel of love, the touch of it, helped them to have life after birth.

A second way to express love is through talk. One of the families I interviewed who had done an absolutely great job in raising their children said: "We covenanted together when we married that we'd not let a day go by without saying to each other, 'I love you.' And when our children were born we agreed that they would not have a day go by without hearing from us those words: 'I love you.'" That wasn't the total secret to their family success, but it contributed a great deal. "I love you" is the most wonderful sentence a person can hear. Coupled with touch, it adds zest to life after birth.

The third way love is expressed is through attitude. Most of us can sense when someone likes or dislikes us; we don't need words or touch—although they make the message clearer. I really don't know how it works, but I have experienced nonverbal communication often with my wife. I have come in late when she's in bed. The room is absolutely dark. Thinking her to be asleep, I sneak in very quietly in order not to disturb her, crawl in bed, and relax to go to sleep. Gradually, I become aware that she is awake although there is no movement or sound to indicate she is. I just feel it. Often I can even tell whether she is in a happy mood or an agitated one. Haven't you been in circumstances where you realize that without visual, audio, or tactile sensation, communication is taking place? It is important for parents to keep an attitude of love and acceptance toward their children. They can sense how parents feel.

A fourth way love is expressed is through action—doing thoughtful, helpful things to show you care, to demonstrate you are aware of a child's needs, interests, and concerns. Actions communicate love: taking time from a busy schedule to play a game or read a story with a child; listening carefully when a child talks about a victory, a defeat, a problem; preparing a youngster's favorite food; working with a youth on a special project. Such actions say, "I'm glad you are part of our family. You're someone special. I love you."

Love should be expressed in all four ways, but often it is not. And children suffer. One weekend during a family life conference in a church I stressed the importance of love. After the conference was over I went to the pastor's office and was gathering my stuff together to leave when I looked up and saw a huge man standing in the door. Redheaded, hands as big as hams, he shook his fist at me and shouted: "You have ruined my family!" I thought to myself, *What a glorious end to a family life emphasis!* I began looking for another door, but the pastor's office was badly designed. There wasn't any way out except through the window. With both flight and fight out of the question, I started trying to cool him off: "Why don't you sit down and let's talk this over?"

He began to share with me how he never did any of the things I'd talked about. Never did he say to his children that he loved them. Never did he hug them. Never did he show any affection. He said, "I don't want to turn them into a bunch of softies. They know I love them because I put food on the table, clothes on their bodies, and a roof over their heads." About that time I heard "thump," "thump," "thump" outside the window and looked out to see a husky redheaded boy with a stick in his hand banging the fronts of all the automobiles parked by the church. The man looked out of the window and said, "That's him. That's my kid. I don't know what I am going to do with him. He's always getting into trouble."

Suddenly the pieces began to fall into place. The scene took on meaning: the child with the stick saying "Dad, pay some attention to me; Dad, love me; Dad, talk to me." I said to the father, "Look, I don't want to tell you what to do, but on the way home why don't you pull that little fellow over against you and say: 'Son, daddies are human, and we make mistakes sometimes. I think I've been making one. I want you to know (and give him a big hug) I think you are something special. I love you.' Then repeat that often in the weeks ahead." I've never seen the two again, but I think that if the father did what I suggested, it made a big difference.

The second ingredient for effective parenting is supervision. Parents guide many aspects of a child's development; three essential ones are self-image, decision-making ability, and skills for daily life.

Few things are more important for life after birth than a positive, realistic self-image. If we don't like ourselves, we probably won't like other people. Apparently the way a child sees himself is partly determined by genetic factors, but in the main the key factor is the way he is treated by others, especially parents. A child who grows up with parents ridiculing him, making fun of him, comparing him unfavorably to others, and telling him how he falls short will probably never develop a good self-image. You've seen the type of "I'm not worth anything" child who is part of that kind of family.

Although a child may not be ridiculed, nothing he does is ever quite right to his parents; praise always carries a cutting undertone. A child brings a model airplane to show to his dad. Proud of his work, he says, "What do you think about that, Dad?" His father glances at the plane and mumbles, "Well, it's all right; but the rudder is a little crooked and you sure got the paint sloppy on the wing, didn't you?" Or a girl comes in from a softball game and asks, "How did I do, Dad?" "Well, you sure flubbed that fly, didn't you?" She caught fifteen others and dropped only one, but the dad talks about the one she dropped.

Supervision is the way a child develops the self-image God wants him to have. That's one of the reasons why God gave children parents. A child's self-image takes a terrible beating in the growing-up process; failures are common; defeats show up daily. Children need parental encouragement, assurance they are OK in spite of the failures.

Decision-making ability is also developed under supervision. Many people grow up not knowing how to make decisions. Have you ever eaten in a restaurant with someone who hasn't learned to make decisions? They look and look at the menu. Then they ask, "What are you going to get?" You tell them and they order something else. When it comes they look at your food and say, "Oh, I wish I had gotten that." Some people find decision making very difficult and never seem happy with the decisions they make. Unless they are guided in learning how to make decisions, they never really know how. They are doomed to having others decide for them or to being unhappy with the choices they make. At best every decision will involve a time of anxiety and agony.

Studies of unwed mothers reveal an interesting thing about them and decision making. Many girls who get pregnant out of wedlock are from families who are either overpermissive ("We trust you; go ahead and do what you want") or overstrict ("We'll tell you what to do; don't you question our judgment").

In either case the girl has not been helped to learn to make decisions. The person who can't make choices is putty in the hands of anybody who is manipulative or domineering. A child needs the kind of guidance in decision making that only a parent can give.

Skills for daily life are also learned by children under parental supervision—how to eat, dress, and speak properly; how to utilize time effectively; how to cope with defeat and disappointment; how to handle pressure and conflict. The list of needed skills is practically endless. There are three types of supervision for skill development. One is the lecture method: "Let me tell you how to do it." The second is example: "Let me show you how to do it." The third is learning by doing: "Let's do it together. Let's study the Bible together. Let's fix the toaster together. Let's repair the car together. Let's wash the dog together." The lecture method is helpful, and example is fruitful; but learning by doing is best. Jesus used all three methods with the disciples: He talked to them. He lived before them. He ministered and worked with them. A parent should use all three also.

In our family we've tried to guide our children through involving them in the pressures of family life. When we faced the decision of leaving a wonderful pastorate to become part of Golden Gate Baptist Seminary, our children were involved. They met with committees, talked over the situation, and had input. They were aware of the difficulties in such a choice and how we were trying to deal with them. I was very proud of my fourteen-year-old daughter, who, when asked about her feelings during a meeting with seminary trustees, replied, "Well, I told God I didn't want to leave Wichita Falls, but if that's what he wanted me to do I would." There is a learning by doing—by going through the process—for which there is no substitute.

The third factor necessary if a child is to have life after birth is discipline. The Old and New Testaments contain instructions about discipline. It is the negative side of child development. Supervision is positive; discipline is negative. Both are very important.

Effective discipline has certain key features. One is that it is for the benefit of the child and not for the emotional release of the parent. Many parents use discipline as an opportunity to vent frustrations. We don't strike out at other adults for fear they will retaliate. The pressure builds, and we subconsciously look for a safe way to vent our frustrations. Then a child violates a rule, and we use this as an opportunity to relieve the pressure by overreacting—yelling, hitting, crying. Many a child becomes a kind of lightning rod, drawing the fire of parental frustration.

The mother of one of the families I interviewed told me, "You know, I learned early that you really have to make sure that what you do under the label of discipline is for the benefit of the child. One day our son walked into the kitchen and said, 'Mama, guess what I've found.' I turned around and saw a frog in his hands. My scream scared the frog, and he hopped into the batter of the cake I was making and right out again. We chased the frog through the house. He splattered batter everywhere and broke a good lamp. Finally we caught the frog and put it in the yard. I thought, *I feel like killing him.* (The boy, not the frog!)

"I sat on the steps and prayed that God would give me strength not to lose control of this situation. I knew that if I lashed out at him now, he might not bring anything else to share with me. He wanted to share. He wasn't being bad. If I punished him, that wonderful desire to share would be stifled. So I said to my son: 'Listen, I really appreciate your wanting to share your discoveries with me, but there are certain things that are better left in the yard. Next time you find something that is alive, call me out, and we will share it together.'

"A few days later I found him doing something I had told him absolutely never to do. He had managed to pry off the protector from an electric receptacle and was beginning to probe it with a fingernail file. At that time I calmly, but forcefully, administered corporal punishment. He had to learn not to violate rules made for his protection." She distinguished between what was for the benefit of the parent and what was for the development of the child.

A second feature of discipline ought to be effectiveness. What is effective depends upon the child. Some children can be put in thumbscrews and on the rack and still refuse to change their destructive patterns. Others you can merely look at with an eyebrow raised as a sign of disapproval and they go into fits of repentance. The form of discipline depends upon the child, but it must be effective. The child must know what the punishment is for. The punishment must be in keeping with the offense. Consistency is essential.

Good discipline leads to self-discipline. A child growing up should ultimately take over disciplinary responsibilities and handle them on his own. Then when he goes to college, the military, or work, he will have self-discipline. The end of discipline should be self-discipline. An inner voice should take over the parents' "Do this" or "Don't do that."

The fourth ingredient is orderliness. Orderliness doesn't call for having everything in its place, although there is nothing wrong with that; rather, it is a way to live in a kind of rhythm: a time to play, a time to work, a time to weep, a time to laugh, a time to worship, and a time to relax. Many families lack that rhythm; and, as a result, it is not built into the children. A workaholic father tends to produce a workaholic son; and a lethargic, apathetic mother tends to produce that kind of a daughter. Parents have a responsibility to help children build rhythm into life.

The fifth ingredient called for in a family if a child is to have life after birth is a sense of togetherness. That doesn't mean physically being together all the time. You can be together physically and not really experience togetherness. A family can cluster around a television set and not be together. Togetherness is a sense of belonging which family members feel. A family has togetherness when they hold common beliefs, practice certain family rituals, and have similar goals. Togetherness comes by playing together, talking together, working together, and praying together. Togetherness can't be developed if family members are never with each other. With a hundred different forces pulling families apart, it is necessary to schedule time together as a family and then protect that schedule.

Togetherness is helped by an awareness of family history. Part of this is achieved by talking about ancestors, tracing family beliefs, practices, and traditions back through several generations. A visit to the family graveyard provides an opportunity to talk about former family members and what they believed in. Going through old family pictures affords a similar opportunity. Our house has a room with a gallery of pictures of family members—past and present.

Family togetherness is also developed through rituals: the way you say good night and good-bye; the way you eat together; the way you celebrate holidays. Holidays provide a special opportunity for ritual by having certain things that are always done at Thanksgiving, Christmas, Easter, the Fourth of July, and other similar days.

The sixth ingredient for life after birth is security. Security is really a by-product. Love brings security, and so does discipline. The worst thing apart from not having love is not having discipline; a child feels his parents don't care enough to go to the trouble to discipline. Supervision contributes to security. A child feels secure with parents who take time to guide and nurture him. A strong sense of togetherness makes a child comfortable in the security of belonging to a group of people who like being together.

Parents can build a sense of security by talking openly

about problems but avoiding expressions of despair about dealing with them. Some parents talk as if they are on the verge of bankruptcy all the time. Dad says, "I just don't know how we're going to make it this year. Prices are up; income's not. It's just terrible." When the family eats out, Dad looks at the menu. "Yipe! At these prices we can't afford to eat!" On shopping trips the children hear, "We're going broke buying clothes; we'll never survive; you kids are going to have to quit growing." With such talk children begin to feel insecure and perhaps even guilty.

Fights between husband and wife can lead to insecurity too. Children fear that their parents are going to get a divorce. Arguments and spats should be interpreted to them. They need to see their parents showing affection for each other. It makes a child feel secure to see Mother and Dad hug and kiss and to hear them express love for each other. In such a setting the parents can say to the children, "We sometimes fuss and fight in this family and even say things we don't really mean, but we're going to stay together."

The seventh ingredient for life after birth is worship. Worship evokes a sense of awe about life, not taking it for granted but realizing that God has given us the gift of life and of family. Worship ought to be a part of every day, not just Sunday. Sunday worship is usually formal; it can be fun, but worship during the week is the kind the whole family can get involved in. Some of our best worship experiences as a family have been when our children have planned family worship.

Worship is one of the things human beings are for, what we were created to do. A person may be too young or old for work, but not for worship. People who learn to worship— to adore, praise, celebrate, enjoy God—have learned one of the chief ingredients of life. People who don't learn to worship never really live. By not knowing God we miss life's most enriching communication. Without the awe experienced by coming into the presence of the King of kings and Lord of lords, life is bland. Risk your life in daredevil stunts, climb the highest mountain, listen to great music perfectly performed, view the most splendid art, win the championship game—do them all and you will not come close to the wonder, the thrill, the impact of true worship.

A child's parents may teach him about history, culture, finance, athletics, and a hundred other items; but unless they teach him to worship, he is a deprived child. Parents may give a child fine clothes, expensive cars, exotic trips, and a luxurious house; but if they do not show him how to worship, they have cheated him of life's richest possession. Worship is a family affair, not something to be left to the professional religionists. Worship experiences are the most precious gifts parents can give children.

What are you doing to see that there will be life after birth for your children? If these seven essentials for life sound familiar to you as a child of God, they should. Jesus spoke often of God as Father. Clearly the relation of God, our heavenly Father, to us, his children, should be a pattern for parents relating to their children.

The Father loves us. He loves us in spite of our sin. He loves us so much that he gave his son so that we could have life after birth through faith in him. He loves us in a thousand ways, touching us with the warm beauty of his creation, speaking in the Bible to us about his love, surrounding us with love through the Holy Spirit.

The Father supervises our growth in Christ; he guides us to maturity. Because he sent his only begotten Son to die and live for us, we learn that we are worth a great deal, that we are special. Through his Word he teaches us how to live. By surrounding us with a family of faith known as a church, he provides persons to guide us in learning life's skills. Through his Son he shows us the example of life as it ought to be. Through his Spirit he works with us, helping us to learn and to grow.

The Father disciplines us, correcting and punishing so that we can find life at its best. What child of God hasn't experienced the discipline of the Father? The terrible agony of guilt, the sting of rebuke, the panic of shame, the suffering of a not-properly-cared-for body—God uses many methods to discipline. His goal is self-discipline.

The Father surrounds us with orderliness. He has built a rhythm into the seasons, into the steady alternation of day and night, into the ebb and flow of the tide. He has ordered a time for planting and a time for harvesting, a time for rejoicing and a time for weeping. As part of the family of God we live in a world of order, an example for our own families.

The Father provides us with a sense of togetherness. He's given us a common destiny, a set of familiar rituals, symbols to unite us, goals to guide us. He teaches us to call one another brother and sister. We share a love for the stories about God's people who lived in the past as well as for the promises about the future. Wherever we go in the world, when we meet Christians we experience togetherness as part of the same family.

The Father makes us feel secure in his family. Have you noticed how often Jesus talked about God's power? about his ability to take care of us? how frequently he emphasized that because God loved us and had all power, we could trust him? Jesus' teachings give us a sense of security. We don't have to fear life or death; God promises to be with us always, to care for us no matter what happens.

The Father has led his family in worship. He's built into us a sense of awe in the presence of the holy. He instructed his people, Israel, in ways of worship—to come before his presence with praise and singing, to celebrate his mighty acts, to enjoy his love and care.

We can't improve on the pattern of parenting that our Father in heaven provides. Neither can we follow his examples on our own. We need his help. There is life after birth only for those who believe in Jesus Christ as Lord and Savior; only they have the divine help needed for abundant life. Similarly, life after birth comes to those children whose parents know and follow God's will, who seek his help. Every parent needs to be a Christian. Every parent ought to pray, "Heavenly Father, help me as a human parent to follow the example set by you, the Divine Parent."

4

The Three Stages of Man

I write unto you, little children, because your sins are forgiven you for his name's sake.

I write unto you, fathers, because ye have known him that is from the beginning. I write unto you, young men, because ye have overcome the wicked one. I write unto you, little children, because ye have known the Father.

I have written unto you, fathers, because ye have known him that is from the beginning. I have written unto you, young men, because ye are strong, and the word of God abideth in you, and ye have overcome the wicked one (1 John 2:12–14).

Recently I was looking over some pictures out of our family archives—early school pictures, high school snapshots, college photographs. It's difficult to realize that the fellow in the picture above the name "Bill Pinson" is really me. Have you ever had such an experience: looking at a picture taken quite awhile ago, wondering, "Who is that stranger with my name?" It makes you aware that life goes through different stages—childhood, youth, adulthood. How amazing that I, a father, was once the baby, the child, the youth in those pictures.

Our language displays an awareness of the stages of man. A child smears oatmeal on the kitchen wall, and Mother says to Daddy, "Don't worry about it; he is just going through a stage." Or a man comes home driving a bright, colorful sporty automobile and his wife says to the children, "Don't worry about it; he's just going through his second childhood." People talk about the springtime of childhood, the summer of youth, the autumn of middle age, and the winter of old age. The divinely inspired writing of 1 John spells out the stages of life—childhood, youth, and adulthood.

We are discovering that within each of these broad stages there are many phases or stages, that life is never really constant, that it is always in flux, constantly changing. Periods of transition are usually difficult for the person going through them as well as for the people who are most intimately related to him.

When child development experts began to explore how a child progresses from birth through the first eight to ten years of life, they discovered and recorded predictable patterns of change. Charts were developed showing typical skills and personality traits of certain ages. Many a parent dashes to his book on child development to see if his child is on schedule. If the child is behind, the parents fret, worry, and try to prod him, speed him up. If the child is ahead of schedule, they boast about it to friends and relatives. The process of grading begins early in life.

The charters of child development discovered an interesting fact. Progress is not steady. There are periods of rapid change and periods of little change. Periods of relative calm are followed by times of disintegration and crisis. Life periodically comes apart and then falls in place once again. We know that during certain phases children come apart at the seams—and their parents do so along with them. Normally there follows a period of stability and relative peace.

When the scholars began to study adolescents, they found a similar pattern. Puberty, it was learned, was not so much a single phase as a series of phases. Teenagers, adolescents, young people—whatever you term them—go through different stages or phases; and these are marked by the same pattern of falling apart and coming back together again observed in childhood. Periods of relative tranquility are followed by periods of chaotic upheaval.

Having traced the patterns of development through adolescence, many of the experts stopped charting. It was assumed that once a person launched into adulthood, having made it through the stormy period of youth, everything was pretty well set. Life was more or less predictable. Many were aware of certain basic changes in middle and old age, of course. But these were mainly matters for jokes, not serious study. Recently widespread, serious study has been undertaken on the phases of adulthood. It is now clear that just as there are different stages among children and youth, there are various phases among adults; life is by no means on a level plane from the twenties onward. The passages into middle age and retirement are only two among many for adults. For years people knew there was a big transition that took place at retirement. And people talked about being over the hill at forty, but few were prepared for what is being discovered— that through *all* of life there are periods of disintegration and integration. Entire families, not just individuals, are affected by these passages from one stage to another.

The Bible teaches that all of life has its stages and that every stage is important. No stage of development ought to be slighted by the people of God. Some have made the mistake of majoring only on adolescence or adulthood. They consider children cute but relatively unimportant and don't spend much time with them. "Children are to be seen and not heard" was the old adage that resulted in many children growing up without the concerted attention necessary for their healthy development. The truth is that by the time a child reaches adolescence, the basic behavior patterns are already established; the personality is already essentially formed. Some parents major on business, church, or community activities while their children are young, depending upon the years of youth for involvement and interaction with them. But when they attempt to relate to their children as youth they discover they don't really know them. They can't seem to get involved with them; there is no bridge between the generations—and there never will be. It is difficult and painful to tell the parent of an adolescent whose behavior pattern is abnormal, "You should have been concerned about him earlier; there is really not much you can do now. You're too late."

Another mistake some Christians make is to feel that the childhood and the youth periods are all that really count, that somehow if we major on those years we can trust the adult years to take care of themselves. The typical church program is an illustration of this attitude. Many churches have preschool, children, and youth directors. They constantly have special programs, camps, and activities for children and teenagers. But for adults it's sink or swim! The attitude seems to be, "We've taken care of you for all these years; now you can take care of yourself. By now you should know what to do, so do it." It's not that adults have been ignored by churches. Sunday School classes, Church Training groups, music programs, and mission organizations are adult-oriented. But compared to the special emphases for children and youth geared to narrow age levels and particular needs, adult programs are usually minimal.

Many churches are now discovering the need to minister to persons of every stage. It is not enough to concentrate on the children and the youth; adults of all ages need attention too. Some churches are building programs and staffs around adult ministry—young adult, middle adult, senior adult, single adult. Others are fashioning ministries around adult-oriented functions—evangelism, spiritual growth, ministry, Christian social action, and family enrichment. Church after church is entering the deacon family ministry program. Deacons and persons working with them are trained to help families and then are given a number of families in the church to care for. Every deacon is offered the opportunity to become a part of a ministry to all stages of family and personal development. It's a way a church can say, "We believe that every stage in life is important. We'll be concerned about all ages and all phases."

If you're asked by your church to accept such a responsibility, I trust you'll realize the importance of it and not shrug it aside, saying, "That's not my work, not my task. That's the pastor's job." If a church ministers to all persons in all stages of life, it's every mature Christian's job; everybody has a responsible place to fill. God indicates that all his children are gifted; he bestows on us the gifts of ministry—to touch a family with concern, to be sensitive to need, to marshal the resources necessary to cope with a particular crisis. When the people of God become truly a family with its members ministering to each other, then we shall all make it through the stages of life in far better condition. Persons and families will be strengthened; society will gain stability.

A deacon came by one night to take me to visit a family in difficulty, one of "his families." He knew each member by name. He knew their birthdays. He'd been by to see them often, not to ask for anything or promote any programs but just to show he cared. Now they were in trouble: wife against husband, parents against children. He knew each one—young and old. He sensed the level of hurt of each. He listened and then shared. I observed. What I observed was a minister in action. The family was helped; so was I. On the way home he said, "Thank you for leading me to this responsibility. Learning how to help families has helped me—and helped my family." That's the way family enrichment works: Those who help are probably helped most of all.

The Bible indicates that all the stages of life are interrelated. Childhood merges into youth and youth into adulthood. Fathers and mothers were once children and youth; there is no way to separate what was from what is. Life is like a river; whatever happens upstream affects what happens downstream. A father is the kind of father he is primarily because of the kind of child and youth he was. You don't change your basic nature as you grow older; you only become more of the same. That is a disturbing truth. Many keep waiting for a magic moment when they will step across the threshold of another year and somehow time will transform them. But time transforms no one. Personality does not grow better with age.

Character does not improve with the passing of year. The grace of God, the ministry of a Christian family, fellowship with other Christians, and discipleship—these are what can transform life. We are basically what we have been, and we are becoming what we are going to be. Look at yourself in the mirror and ask the question, "Do I want to be this kind of person the rest of my life?" If not, enter into a partnership with God for change—now! Life is so interrelated that your next phase will be much like this one unless you take direct action to bring about change.

Childhood begins the process and is of basic importance. The way a child is molded affects what kind of adult he becomes. In God's design the influence of the home is the method for shaping character. In God's plan parents are more basic for personality formation than conversion. Perhaps, therefore, in concentrating on children we have missed the point; we have neglected the parents who are the molders of children's lives. If we have not helped them parent in the very best way possible, we have contributed to an adverse effect on children.

A church may do well with children the few hours they are involved in such things as Sunday School; but unless the parenting process is strengthened too, we have not done all we should. A child doesn't stand much of a chance to grow up wholesome and healthy according to the pattern of God unless his family is wholesome, healthy, and well integrated. A Sunday School session and youth retreat now and then are better than no Christian influence at all, but are certainly no substitute for a well-functioning Christian family. The interrelatedness of the stages of man which the Scriptures describe calls us to total ministry.

The Bible also indicates that each stage has its own characteristics. The Scripture speaks of childhood as the stage best known for innocence and trust. Youth is known for its vigor, its ability to overcome difficulties. The Bible speaks of the fathers, the mature adults, as best known for their wisdom and knowledge. That children are basically innocent and trusting doesn't mean they are naturally good, but they are more trusting and less cynical than most adults. Youth is a time of vigor, dreaming, activity, and energy. Old age is a time of reflection. We all know that. But sometimes we know it too well and we insist that people fit totally the characteristics of their stage in life.

Have you ever seen a parent speaking harshly to a somber, serious child? "Don't be such an old man." Well, there are times when a child needs to be an "old man," serious, in deep thought, and reflecting. Or have you ever heard somebody say to an older person, "Don't be so childish"? Sometimes that means the person is acting selfishly, pouting, and shouting. But that is not behaving childishly; that is behaving badly. Unfortunately, older persons are sometimes termed childish when they kick up their heels, play practical jokes, have a lot of fun. Some people think that fun is only for little kids. They are wrong. Fun is for everybody; play is for everyone; frolic is for all ages—just as somberness and seriousness are for all ages.

Let's not get life so neatly categorized—let's not follow the development charts so thoroughly—that we force everyone to display characteristics that we feel are acceptable to certain stages, ages, and phases. Let's realize that everyone has a little child in him and everyone has an old man in him; that everyone ought to exercise the responsibility and stability usually identified with the middle years of adulthood. It is true that different characteristics are highlighted in different stages in keeping with God's plan for life. But these characteristics don't belong exclusively to any one age, stage, or phase.

The Bible also teaches that the characteristics of the Christian life follow a different growth pattern from that of physical and personality development. You can predict rather accurately the physical development of a person from infancy to childhood to adolescence to adulthood to middle adulthood to old age. You can even predict with some degree of certainty the development of skills during those years. But in the Christian life the characteristics described by the Bible for the different stages are not attached to years. Upon first reading what John said, you may think that the Scripture is speaking of physical stages. He addressed little children, young men, and fathers. But more careful attention reveals that it couldn't be that way because the same characteristics attributed to fathers are also attributed to children—"ye have known the Father" (v. 13). Here is a marvelous truth. God equips us with the characteristics of various stages all at once. The Christian is to have the best attributes of a child, a youth, and an adult.

We begin the Christian life as a child. Jesus said, "Whosoever shall not receive the kingdom of God as a little child, he shall not enter therein" (Mark 10:15). It is with childlike faith and trust that we come to know God's love and forgiveness. When we give up our sense of self-sufficiency, when we realize we don't have the strength and power to live on our own, when we acknowledge that we are as dependent as an infant—then God's mercy and grace can operate in our lives. As long as we function as a self-sufficient adult with an "I can take care of this myself, thank you!" attitude, there is no salvation. We can be saved from the power and penalty of sin only when we confess we are sinners and are helpless—helpless as an infant to care for itself—to deal with the sin and depend totally on God for salvation. New life in Christ begins at the point of childlike faith, of an acknowledgment of dependence, of total and complete helplessness. "God, help me, I cannot help myself; forgive me, I cannot forgive myself; save me, I cannot save myself." Childlike trust does not end with conversion. It is not limited to one stage in the Christian life. The Christian is to be childlike during all of life in trust, faith, and dependence on God the Father.

The Bible teaches that every Christian is to have the vigor of youth. Youth who are strong in the Word of God "overcome the wicked one" (v. 14). In physical life youth is the time of strength, daring, and activity. In the Christian life, these characteristics are to be present in every believer. The war against Satan is not just for the young; it is for older people and children as well. Children wage the battle against Satan. Older people wage the battle against Satan. What the Scripture promises is that each Christian, regardless of chronological age, has access to strength in the Word of God to overcome the Evil One. All Christians armed with the Word of God can take the battle to the enemy. Retired persons can travel to distant places, live on retirement incomes, and help share the gospel. Children can bear witness at school and play. Youth can share Christ in the midst of a multitude of activities.

Adulthood is a time of knowledge; years of schooling and experience provide adults with knowledge necessary to tackle many responsible tasks. But the knowledge of God is the most important knowledge. It alone makes one truly wise. Although you are a brilliant scientist, knowing all there is to know about nuclear physics, if you do not know God you are not wise concerning the order of the universe. Although you are a brilliant historian, knowing all the dates and facts of history, if you do not know God you are basically ignorant about the meaning of history. Although you are a businessman, knowing all about trade, investments, and finance, if you do not know God you are basically foolish about wealth. Whether a child, a young person, or an adult, the Christian possesses the greatest wisdom of all, the wisdom that comes from the knowledge of God.

The knowledge of God is available at all the stages of life. When the Scriptures speak of knowing God, the emphasis is not on knowing about him but on knowing him personally. Knowing God does not mean primarily knowing a great many facts about him, but sharing life with him, giving oneself to him, fellowshipping with him, being committed to him. In that way, a child can know God just as well as a grandparent can.

At each stage in life you need the resources God provides. You will find life at its best when you possess all the attributes of the various phases of the Christian life. Are you trusting God to save you and keep you, trusting with a childlike faith? Are you drawing strength daily from the Word of God and overcoming the wicked one with the daring and vigor of youth? Are you growing in your knowledge of God and developing the wisdom of mature adulthood? At whatever stage, in whatever phase, live it with God. God gave his Son to die and live for you; trust him to forgive and save you. God gave his Word to guide and strengthen you; read, study, and memorize the Bible so that it abides in you. God reveals himself to you; learn of him and come to know him. Therein is life—in all its stages.

When all the persons in a family, in each of its stages, are experiencing life abundant in God the Father through Jesus the Son, then that family will experience life abundant. The key to a stable, joyful, meaningful family life is for life in all its stages to be rooted firmly in God. Just as the phases of life are interrelated, the members of a family are interrelated. The life of one affects the life of all. Won't you make your life—at whatever stage you are—Christ-centered? Only you can do that. Your family, as well as you, will then begin to taste the abundant life that Jesus promised.

5

Midcourse Correction

Thou shalt not be afraid for the terror by night; nor for the arrow that flieth by day; Nor for the pestilence that walketh in darkness; nor for the destruction that wasteth at noonday (Ps. 91:5–6).

What is the best time in the life of a family? Is it the first years when marriage is new, life is fresh, children are young, dreams are big, and energy is high? Is it the middle years when children are out of diapers and able to relate as human beings, some degree of comfort and security is enjoyed, a routine has been established, and experience makes life flow more smoothly? Or is it the latter years when children are gone and a couple can concentrate on each other, the enormous expense of childrearing and college education is past, pressures are less, and there's time for reflection?

When is the worst time in the life of a family? Is it during the first years when income is low and expenses are high, when children are demanding and constantly sick, when husband and wife are trying to adjust to each other and to a new style of life? Is it the middle years when life settles into a bland routine, children are leaving the nest, the zest seems to have gone out of life, and pressures and frustrations are great? Or is it the latter years when serious illness comes surging in like the pounding surf, health fades and friends die, retirement approaches, and one's children suffer disappointment, loss, and unhappiness?

Clearly each stage in the life of a family has its good features and bad. At each stage families need help. Yet most of the help seems to be directed toward the earlier and later years. Sermons, books, articles, and programs abound on helping young adults establish marriages and parent children. In recent years an avalanche of material has tumbled from various sources to help the aging family. But for those in the middle years, the resources are meager and the help is small.

Part of the neglect results from a common attitude that people in the middle years have the resources to cope with life's difficulties. They possess the experience lacking in youth without suffering the incapacities of old age. But the psalmist, himself likely in the middle years, knew the difficulties of midlife. He speaks of "the destruction that wasteth at noonday" (Ps. 91:6) in the middle of life. He had seen it in King Saul, who in his younger years was a man of strength and vigor but who in his middle years suffered emotional and mental collapse. He had seen it in his own life. As a youth David had been of sterling quality, but in the middle years he fell prey to lust which led to adultery. He may have sensed it in his son, Solomon, who, though a wise young man, suffered in his middle years the dissipation of sensuality and materialism.

It takes only a glance at families in the noonday of life to know that many are being destroyed. In fact, the marital landscape looks almost like a battlefield, littered by broken families in middle years. Divorce rates are high in these years. The delinquency of older children breaks up family stability. Emotional and physical collapse are common. These features of families in the middle years make the headlines, but perhaps the most common plight is that of quiet despair; purpose and vitality go out of a marriage and leave only apathy, routine, and indifference. What is alive on the surface is dead at the heart.

What are the things that destroy families in the middle years? The list is long, according to those who study family life. One of the most common destroyers is emotional, spiritual, and physical overload due to busyness. The family takes on more than it can handle and blows a fuse. Sometimes the overload is a family's own fault. The members of the family try to do too much, engage in too many activities, make too many commitments. More promises are made than there is time to keep them. Stress, strain, guilt, and exhaustion take their toll.

However, some of the overload may be due to a family's natural circumstance in the middle years. These are the bridge years. Parents in the middle years are bridges between their teenage children and their aging parents. Relating to adolescents and to aging adults can be a draining experience emotionally, financially, mentally, and spiritually. If they are not careful, middle-aged parents will have given more than they have to give. The result is collapse.

Further, the middle years are the taffy years. Various persons, groups, and institutions grab for middle-aged parents' time, resources, and skills. Businesses, community groups, churches, civic clubs, schools, and others pull and tug. As a result, middle-aged mothers and fathers, husbands and wives, often feel like bits of taffy pulled this way and that by a multitude of persons and institutions. If they don't learn to resist, the family will be torn apart and fragmented.

Fear is another destructive force for the middle years. Much of the fear centers in change. Change seems omnipresent for the noonday family. Physical changes are evident. For the children the changes herald increased strength, sexual development, virility. Not so for the parents. The body accelerates the aging process. Stamina and strength wane. Although sexual capacity may remain strong, it is not the driving force it was earlier. Often these changes bring emotional turmoil. At the time they need stability and support, middle-aged parents often must cope with the emotional ups and downs of adolescent children and aging parents. An emotionally volatile situation is compounded. This may make a person at the noonday of life fear he no longer has the capacity to cope. The urge to flee, to retreat, is strong. Sometimes the retreat is in the form of an emotional collapse; sometimes a person literally runs away. Runaway parents are more and more common. They resign from parenthood and leave.

Other fears can destroy at noonday. The fear of losing sexual capability and desirability can trigger an affair to prove that one still has sexual capacity and appeal. The fear that a younger person is going to take over one's job can lead to irrational and destructive behavior patterns at work. The fear of losing one's financial security can lead to either miserliness or wild speculation in investments—both of which are likely to destroy sound family life.

Frustration is another destroyer at noonday. Frustration has many causes in the middle years. When children are young, they can be controlled. When they are older, they cannot be. For some parents, the realization that they are losing control of their children causes great frustration. Frustration in one's vocation is also common in the middle years. At midlife many people begin to realize that the dreams of youth are not going to be fulfilled. Fenced in, trapped by circumstances, with time running out, they know they are not going to achieve their goals. Such a realization can lead to serious depression. To compound the difficulty, many are embarrassed because they have not lived up to expectations others have for them—parents, spouse, children, friends. If a spouse or children nag and complain because of lack of achievement, the frustration level can become practically unbearable.

Getting into a rut also destroys families at the noonday of life. Many middle-aged couples have settled into a groove. The word *grave* has the same root as the word *groove*. They are similar. A groove is a grave with both ends knocked out. Getting into a rut spells the end of vitality in marriage. Sameness can bring dullness. Every day brings more of the same. If persons in the midyears are not careful, they will stop dreaming and cease exploring new experiences. They will grow dull and boring. They will not enjoy being with each other or with others. Their children will want to leave home early and come back to visit seldom.

Materialism and greed can be destroyers at noonday. These vices are not limited to persons in the middle years, but people often get consumed by materialism at this time of life. They destroy health, family, and personal relationships in a mad pursuit for things. To make the matter even worse, when they do achieve material success they usually find it is not what they thought it would be. It brings little satisfaction, and they worry about keeping what they have accumulated.

A Christian millionaire told me, "The two saddest days of my life, I think, were the day my accountant told me I was bankrupt and the day he told me I was a millionaire. Bankruptcy did not materialize, but I was concerned about my family and what people would think if I went broke. When he told me I was a millionaire, I drove home thinking, *Is this what I've worked for? There's no real joy in having achieved it.*" During the middle years it is important to remember that one's purpose is not to make a living but to make a life, that a family's material needs ought to be provided for but that money and things do not bring happiness. A person should do well whatever work he believes is God's will for his life and let financial compensation come as it may.

An outstanding college president at the noonday of life told me recently, "My goal is not to get rich. I have limited goals; my dad taught me that. I want to provide for my family and for my retirement. Beyond that, I've got more important things to do than to make money for money's sake." It is not by accident that he is part of a fine Christian family.

Pride is another destroyer at noonday. Many people in middle age have achieved some success. They have developed talent and ability. They often rest on their laurels, trust in their own resources, and believe they are really self-made. Living by sight and not by faith, they stumble into the pit of pride. Believing themselves to be self-sufficient, they cut off their link not only with God but with others. They dry up spiritually and relationally. They suffer—and their families suffer with them.

Preoccupation and separation are common destroyers at noonday. A husband and wife become preoccupied with their own activities. Each may have separate careers, separate sets of friends, separate interests. Before long, they're living separate lives. They have no real link between them and marriage becomes a farce. They drift apart, lose contact with each other, and wake up one day to the knowledge that they don't even know one another. A similar pattern happens in relation to children. Middle-aged parents may become so caught up in their careers, civic activities, church, or club that they lose communication with children. A common cry I hear from young people is, "I can't talk to my parents. They're hardly ever home. When they are, they don't really listen to me."

Many families at noonday are on a collision course with destruction. They are like an off-course airplane about to run out of fuel and crash in the wilderness. They need a midcourse correction. Such families need to rediscover their purpose, head toward the goals God has for them, and avoid destruction at noonday.

The midcourse correction relates partly to the individuals involved in the family. Middle-aged husbands and wives (who are usually also parents) need to acknowledge their mortality, the limits of their strength, and their dependence upon God. By being realistic about ability and strength, by pacing oneself and accepting only what can be done within one's limits, and by carefully defining goals, much of the frustration, over-load, and weariness of the noonday years can be avoided. Further, people in the middle years should make plans, dream about the future, and catch a vision from God about the rest of their life.

The relation of husband and wife may call for midcourse correction. Up until this time the race has usually been frantic. Communication between husband and wife may have practi-cally ceased because they were running so fast that there has been little time for personal relationships. The noonday years often call for getting reacquainted with one's spouse. Hus-bands and wives need to prepare for the next stage—the empty nest and retirement. They ought to discover who each other really is now. With the passing of years, personalities have altered. Many couples in midlife need to rediscover the joy and spontaneity of sexuality. They need to establish communication by laughing together, talking together, dreaming together, planning together, praying together, and discussing together their fears and joys, frustrations, and aspirations. They may need to explore each other's roles because roles and role concepts change as persons grow older.

Relation to children often calls for midcourse correction. The father or mother who in earlier years has been too busy to really get to know children may in the middle years suddenly want to establish a close, warm, personal relationship with them. Persons at middle age often reach out for close personal relationships; people become more important than things or position. But by this time the children have already begun to establish other relationships and may reject the parent's belated efforts at communication. This inability to relate to adolescent and young adult children can lead to anger, hurt, frustration, and grief. What may be called for is establishing a new kind of relationship—adult to adult. As children move out from under the authority of parents, adjustments must be made. Parents in the middle years need to remember that when their children marry, they are to forsake father and mother.

Relation to God is the most important aspect of the midcourse correction. The family at noonday caught up in materialism, pride, busyness, and preoccupation with 1,001 demands needs to change course. God must be given top priority. In a relationship of trust and obedience with the living God rests the major defense against the destroyers at noonday. As the psalmist stated, "I will say of the Lord, He is my refuge and my fortress: my God; in him will I trust" (Ps. 91:2). The psalmist insisted that God was his protection. That same protection is promised to all who will trust in the Most High: "Because thou has made the Lord, which is my refuge, even the most High, thy habitation; There shall no evil befall thee, neither shall any plague come nigh thy dwelling" (Ps. 91:9–10).

For those threatened by the storms of change, peace comes

by trusting in the one who has said, "I am the Lord, I change not" (Mal. 3:6). The changeless God of change comes into one's life not only to furnish stability and a solid point of reference but also to alter and correct, to strengthen and to enhance. Trust in the heavenly Father provides stability in an unstable time, strength when one's own power is weakening, and a sense of values when the temptation to jettison morality is strong.

The family in the middle years faces the specter of the destruction that wasteth at noonday. The only adequate defense is trust in the God who sent his Son, Jesus Christ, to die in order that we might live, to suffer in order that we might know wholeness. By trusting in him, the members of a family at its noonday can avert destruction. By heeding what he says about the home, by following his instructions for family, by setting their priorities in marriage according to his imperatives, their course can be altered from death to life. The rut of the routine can be avoided by walking with him who daily makes everything new. Fear is replaced by faith, frustration by direction, materialism by spiritual wholeness, pride by trust, and destructive overload by decisions deliberately made in the will of God.

The remedy for the destruction that wasteth at noonday is midcourse correction. Won't you begin that correction now? Place your family in the hands of the one who promises salvation and eternal life, protection and joy, adventure and peace, security and purpose. Often I have seen families disintegrating in midcourse, being torn to bits by the destroyers that strike at noonday, turn to a new course set by the will of God. Through faith in Jesus Christ as the Son of God, a person's life begins to center in God's ways. The family now has a purpose, new strength, and stability. Most important, the family has the presence of the living God to protect them against the destruction at noonday. Oh, don't go another day without making him the protector of your family.

6

When You Will Be Old

Verily, verily, I say unto thee, When thou wast young, thou girdest thyself, and walkedst whither thou wouldest: but when thou shalt be old, thou shalt stretch forth thy hands, and another shall gird thee, and carry thee whither thou wouldest not.

This spake he, signifying by what death he should glorify God. And when he had spoken this, he saith unto him, Follow me.

Then Peter, turning about, seeth the disciple whom Jesus loved following; which also leaned on his breast at supper, and said, Lord, which is he that betrayeth thee?

Peter seeing him saith to Jesus, Lord, and what shall this man do?

Jesus saith unto him, If I will that he tarry till I come, what is that to thee? follow thou me (John 21:18–22).

When you are young you don't think much about when you will be old. I doubt if Peter had ever given his old age much thought. Certainly as he stood by the lake talking with Jesus, being old was not his concern. Peter squirmed under Jesus' questioning: "Simon, son of Jonas, lovest thou me?" Twice Peter had declared his love for Jesus. Twice Jesus had commanded Peter to feed his lambs, his sheep.

Then came the question a third time. Three was a touchy number with Peter, for he had three times denied Jesus. He blurted out, "Lord, Thou knowest all things; thou knowest that I love thee." Jesus said unto him, "Feed my sheep" (John 21:17). Picking up on Peter's phrase "Thou knowest all things," Jesus said, "Verily, I say unto thee, When thou art young, thou girdest thyself, and walkedst whither thou wouldest: but when thou shall be old, thou shall stretch forth thy hands, and another shall gird thee, and carry thee whither thou wouldest not." The biblical writer added, "This spake he, signifying by what death he should glorify God. And when he had spoken this, he said unto him, Follow me."

When Peter had this encounter with Jesus he was probably in his late twenties or early thirties, full of vigor, an able-bodied man, strong, and muscular, having never really thought much about a time when he would be old. But there in the midst of the encounter Jesus laid out for Peter his future as an old man. There's no record in the Bible of how Peter died. Tradition has it that he was crucified—not upright, as Jesus was, but upside down because he felt unworthy to be crucified in the same manner as Jesus. Jesus was likely referring to his kind of death when he told Peter how he would die.

Peter could have spent the rest of his life brooding about what Jesus had told him, about how awful the future was going to be, about how when he was old he would be carried about by others and then taken to his death. He could have failed to live his life by worrying about what it would be like when he was old. But he didn't. Rather, he took Jesus at his word and trusted him. He believed that whatever was in store for him, it could glorify God. Therefore, he committed himself to following what God wanted him to do.

The promise of difficulty when we are old should not rob us of living in the present to the fullest. It does for some people, you know. Although we don't know all that the future holds for us when we are old, we're relatively sure that it holds something of what Jesus forecast for Peter: incapacity, inability to move about freely, pain, dependence on others, and death.

Unlike Peter, there are those who are robbed of the joy of life by worrying about what it will be like when they are old. Some who visit hospitals and rest homes, who come face to face with persons who are old and incapacitated, develop fear of old age. Old age for them becomes the most dreaded disease of all. Their thoughts are plagued by anxiety over it. They're afraid that when they're old their health will fail. They'll be confined to bed. Their body will be in pain day and night. They fear the wearing out of body parts and the embarrassment of being dependent on others. They dread financial insolvency, feeling that with runaway inflation their savings will be gone long before life is gone and they'll be poverty-stricken. Or they're concerned that friends will die, family will move away, their mate will perish, and they'll be all alone. Terrified by their expectation of what will happen when they are old, they simply lose their life before they ever live it.

Being old, Jesus told Peter, will be hard, but that should not rob you of service in the present or of the expectation that God will use your condition in the future to glorify his name. Jesus commanded Peter to live a life of ministry: "Feed my sheep." By so living in the present he would prepare for old age in the future. What we are when we are old, how we respond to the trials of aging, depends on what we do with life now. Each of us will be older, regardless of how old we are. What you will be when you are older will be the result of what you do in the present as you move into God's future.

Age is supposed to make some things better. Aged beef is supposed to be tastier than fresh beef. Aged cheese is supposed to be of finer quality than fresh cheese. Fine old furniture is supposed to be better than new furniture. But that's not necessarily true with human life. There's no promise in the Bible that growing older makes us better. None at all. As we grow older we may become better, get worse, or remain the same. What matters is not the age; it's the relationship we have with God and others. It's not the number of our years; it's what we do with our years that affects what we will be when we are older.

Some people think of life as a series of watertight compartments: childhood, adolescence, young adulthood, middle age, senior adulthood, and the last years. They believe you can live within each compartment pretty well the way you want and then open the door and move to the next one, shutting the past behind you. That belief leads some young people to consider sowing their wild oats before settling down. It is used as a basis to explain away sexual looseness by a person who says, "While I'm young I'll enjoy sex with lots of different people; then I'll marry one person and live faithfully and happily the rest of my life." But there's no indication whatsoever in reason or revelation that such is the case. Why should infidelity develop fidelity?

What a person is is what a person becomes. Life is not like a series of watertight compartments; it is like a river. If you pollute the source, you pollute the end. Whatever you drop into a river affects the water downstream. Whatever you drop into life at each point affects what happens to life when you are older.

A person who does not treat his body as the dwelling place of the Holy Spirit, who abuses it through taking drugs, eating too much of the wrong kind of food, or failing to get adequate rest or exercise, will suffer from the damage done to the body. What is sowed is what is reaped. When you are older it is not possible to shut a compartment and move into the next where there is a fresh, new body to inhabit. Rather, you will drag into those older years the body which you have afflicted in the earlier ones.

What is true of your body is true of your mind and attitudes. What you read, experience, listen to, observe, and dwell on becomes part of you for the rest of your life. I've had people tell me: "I want to experience all life has to offer. I want to try everything at least once if I can." I don't. There's no way anyone can experience *all* life has to offer; I want to experience the *best*—the most constructive—life has to offer, partly because by doing the best now I can look forward to living with the results and memories of those good experiences for the rest of my life. Why build in regrets?

Yes, life is like a stream. What you and I will be when we are older is dependent upon what we do right now. That's true in every area of life—finances, health, attitude, behavior, and relationships. You are rapidly becoming the kind of person you are going to be for the rest of your life. A cantankerous, selfish, surly, hard-to-get-along-with eighteen-year-old is likely to be a cantankerous, selfish, surly, hard-to-get-along-with eighty-year-old. There's nothing in the span of life that automatically improves itself.

On the other hand, a generous, happy, fulfilled, God-serving, ministry-oriented middle adult is likely to be that kind of person when he or she grows older. Expect no magic with the passing of years. We will have in the future what we have acquired in the present. The only thing that transforms us is God himself, not age. The only way we can experience the transforming power of God is to open our life to him, to the ministry of his Spirit through faith in his Son, Jesus Christ.

The most important thing we can do to prepare for enjoying the years ahead is to love God and minister to others today. Jesus told Peter: "Love me and feed my sheep." What was good for Peter is good for us. Expanded in meaning, Jesus' command is to spend your days in ministry. Don't live to pile up possessions or honors or power. Don't strive to get a position of prominence over your brethren. Rather, live in ministry and service. Feed my sheep, Peter. If you'll spend your life loving me and feeding my sheep, when you are older you will be blessed beyond measure. If you spend your days in selfish gratification, if you spend your years thinking only of yourself, you'll grow old in a selfish and binding kind of way.

But if you'll live your life in generous giving, if you'll throw yourself into ministry to other people, if you'll consider the world around you as a flock of sheep in need of care, you'll discover that your life grows richer as you give, more meaningful as you share, more dynamic as you serve.

Then Jesus said to Peter: "Follow me." By that he meant, "Do my will. Obey my commandments. Do what I ask. Follow and be like me." Jesus' words to Peter are for us all. How do we prepare for the difficult days ahead? By following Jesus now. When you do, you'll walk into the future not with fear but with hope, for you will have come to know the God who has redeemed us through Jesus Christ, who took a broken body from the cross and made it whole through resurrection, who took the shattered dreams of frightened disciples and molded a future of confident love. "Follow me" is the key to good old age.

The Bible doesn't promise that if you follow Jesus, everything will be perfect when you are older. There's no promise that your health will be good, that your wealth will be large, that your friends will be numerous. No. In fact, Jesus told Peter: "When you are older you will hurt; you will be confined; you will be embarrassed; and you will die." But Jesus also said to him: "You will glorify God if you follow me." You see, what brings God glory and us joy is not our health, our wealth, our friends, or our location. It is whether we are following Jesus Christ or not. If you're following him, then you're finding life at its best. If you're not, you're finding life at its worst.

Follow Jesus and the specters that haunt you, those frightening shadows that cloud the enjoyment of the present, will fade away as the fog before the morning sun. Are you afraid of dying? Death can come at any age. It comes for children; it comes for young people; it comes for middle adults. But it most certainly comes for older adults. As a group, those who are older have fewer years to count on than those who are younger; but we all die.

Those who have followed Jesus are not terrified by death. Those of us who are privileged to stand by the bedsides of people who die, to hold their hands as the last flicker of life goes out, to look into their eyes as they begin to lose focus besieged by death, know that the people who have followed Jesus follow him into the valley of the shadow of death and are not afraid to die. They know he walks with them not simply *into* the valley but *through* it. Oh, it's not that they want to die and it's not that they don't hurt, but there is for them an awareness of the presence of the living Lord. Their fears are eased.

People who follow Jesus are able to handle the pain that so often comes when we are older, whether it's the pain of arthritic disease or of cancer or of body parts wearing out. This isn't true because they hurt less than others. It's because they are aware of the promise of his presence, "Lo, I am with you alway, even unto the end" (Matt. 28:20). It's because they see an opportunity to glorify God, to bear witness to his love. Again and again I've gone to hospital rooms to comfort aging Christians in excruciating pain; and again and again it is I who have been comforted by them, inspired by their calm faith in our heavenly Father.

Why are they able to deal with hurt this way? Perhaps they feel as one woman who, through tears shed involuntarily because of pain, said, "Don't worry about me. All of my life I've wondered what that passage meant, 'the fellowship of his sufferings,' and now I'm beginning to know. As I hurt, I imagine the hurt of my Lord on the cross. As my body is pained, I associate with his pain in dying for my sins. Now more than any other time in my life, I thank God for my salvation."

For those who have begun to experience the loneliness that can come when you are older—when families move away, when people don't seem eager to visit and converse, when hearing begins to weaken, shutting you off from much of daily life—there's the comfort of his promise to be with you. One of my older friends laughingly said several months ago, "I think I'm going to go ahead and hold my funeral right now while there are still some people around who know me!" She was half serious and half joking because almost everyone who had been close to her was dead. She was alone—but not really because she was, in Christ, part of the family of God.

I learned the lesson of how older Christians can handle loneliness from the mother of Billy Graham. One day in Charlotte, North Carolina, I visited her in the home where Billy Graham had grown up. As we chatted in that big old farmhouse I said to her, "It must be awfully lonely living here by yourself." She replied, "Oh, no, not at all. This house is full of memories. But more important than that, my family comes by quite often." I interrupted, "But I thought your family lived quite a distance away." She said, "No, no; I mean my church family. My Sunday School class and my friends. I'm never really alone. And most important, my Lord is with me all the time." As I left I found myself singing softly, "He promised never to leave me,/Never to leave me alone."

The person who follows Jesus discovers that however long life lasts, if he has been faithful to him and to the body of Christ—the church—he possesses the resources to cope with loneliness. It's best to start early in life developing Christian friends and a church relationship. It is almost impossible to cultivate friendships and a church family late in life. A farmer may suddenly realize that he failed to sow seed at the right time. He may plant some later, but it is practically impossible for the crop to come in full. The time to get ready for old age is right now.

The best way to prepare for old age is to follow Jesus, to trust him. Then you don't have to worry about hell when death comes. You know that your home is in heaven, that you are saved, and that your sins are forgiven. By being an active part of a church family while you are younger and by developing many close friendships, you will not have to worry about loneliness and isolation when you are older. You will be part of a family that never goes away. By living a life of Christian ministry, you will come into later years with a sense of enthusiasm because feeding sheep, as Jesus told

Peter to do, is a lifelong venture, one from which you never retire. People who grow old in Christ grow old in a way that those without him do not. Follow Jesus; feed his sheep; and you will glorify God when you're older.

Right now, before you are a moment older, whether you are young or ancient, follow Jesus, trust in the One who loved you and died for you. Put your life in his hands. Begin now the process of growing richer and deeper in his spirit. Then as the river of life moves you toward older years, you will develop the kind of life that will glorify God and bring you happiness. Isn't that what you really want?

7

Becoming Single

Jesus cried with a loud voice, saying, Eli, Eli, lama sa-bach-tha-ni? that is to say, My God, my God, why hast thou forsaken me? (Matt. 27:46).

What kind of person comes to mind when you hear "single adult"? A bachelor deftly dodging marriage? A "swinging single," rootless and sexually uninhibited? An "unclaimed blessing," prim, proper, and set in her ways? A "merry widow" living it up on her husband's hard-earned money? Single adults are not all alike, but the usual stereotypes of singles fit few of them. Singles are difficult to classify. In most ways single adults are like married adults; they vary in regard to age, personality, beliefs, attitudes, and practices. Single adults do, however, fall into two rather distinct groups: the formerly married and the never married. There's a vast difference in *being* single and *becoming* single. It is a mistake to lump all single adults together.

There are millions of unmarried persons for whom *being* single is a way of life. Some are single by choice. Many intend to marry sometime; others feel marriage is not right for them. A number have experienced the hurt of rejection; they are not married because no one has asked them or because those they asked said no. For most the trauma of rejection is not disabling, and they either continue to live in hope of marriage or accept *being* single and develop a life with purpose and meaning. Some never adjust to being single and continue to suffer from a loss—the loss of a relationship that never happened.

75

Becoming single, on the other hand, is quite a different matter. All those who have become single—the formerly married—share a common experience: separation. Through death, divorce, mutual agreement, or abandonment, they have been separated from one with whom they had linked life in love and hope. Those who have been through the ordeal of such separation know how much it hurts.

The Bible's opening chapters reveal how important relation is and how deeply painful separation is. God ministered to Adam by providing someone to whom he could relate. One of God's choice gifts is that of relation. Part of God's punishment imposed on Adam and Eve for their transgression was separation. The best of God's gifts is relation to him and others in love, and the worst of God's penalties is separation.

Jesus identified with us in every way, including experiencing the agony of separation. The most awful cry recorded in human history is that of Jesus from the cross, "My God, my God, why hast thou forsaken me?" More agonizing than his physical pain, more terrible than his disappointment over the disciples, more anguishing than his rejection by his fellow countrymen, was the pain of his separation from the heavenly Father.

Our own experiences affirm the biblical truth about separation and relation. Life's most wonderful moments are found in relationship—love, marriage, parenting, friendship. Life's greatest hurts come from separation—death, divorce, rejection, abandonment. We human beings understand the sting of separation quite well. We use it to mete out punishment: the child is sent to his room alone; the prisoner is put in solitary confinement; the traitor is banished or exiled.

True, separation is a part of life and everyone experiences it. The infant grieves when separated from parents. Husbands and wives grieve when separated from one another. Families grieve when separated from loved ones. Leaving friends is always painful. Yet the kind of separation that leads a person to become what we call a single adult is probably the most painful type of separation. Becoming single means that separation replaces relation, that a person experiences life's most painful emotions, such as rejection, a sense of failure, guilt, grief, anger, anxiety, fear, distrust, and loneliness.

As Christians our role regarding those who suffer separation is not to pity them or to feel sorry for them. Such attitudes are condescending and disabling. Rather, we are to try to understand the effect of separation on them, minister to their needs, and help them put the pieces back together when life falls apart. For those who have not walked the painful path to becoming single, it is difficult to understand what the person who becomes single experiences. Yet we ought to try in order to walk with him as helping friends.

Grief is common to almost all who become single. When part of you is ripped away, it hurts. When you lose someone you have loved, grief is a natural response. Grief follows a relatively predictable pattern. There is shock and numbness, bewilderment and questioning, anger and hostility, withdrawal and depression, and finally—for most anyway—acceptance and beginning again. Grief is part of the price paid for loving. It is a high price to pay, but it is not too high. Life without love is not really life.

Whether separation comes by divorce or death, it brings grief. Most of us are more adept at responding to the grief that results from death than we are the grief that results from divorce. But grief is real in both instances. A friend of mine, a specialist in family life, was interviewing a group of Christians about family ministry. A woman in the group said, "I've lost two husbands, one by death and one by divorce. When I lost my husband by death, friends and church members by the dozens came by to comfort me. When I lost my husband through divorce, no one showed up." Another member of the group exclaimed, "But I wouldn't know what to say!" The woman responded, "They didn't know what to say when I lost my husband through death. The important thing is not what you say but that you are there."

A sense of failure and a feeling of guilt usually accompany separation. At best divorce is failure, and the parties involved know it. They realize they have not succeeded in one of life's most important ventures. Failure always hurts. The person who accepts responsibility for the failure will also experience pangs of guilt. The primary remedy for failure and guilt is acknowledgment of wrong, repentance, confession, and acceptance of forgiveness from God, who has promised that if we will confess our sins he will forgive us and cleanse us from all unrighteousness.

Even when separation comes by death, there is often a sense of failure and guilt on the part of the surviving member of the marriage. The survivor may feel that more adequate medical care should have been sought, that more attention should have been paid to the one who died, or that he is in some way responsible for the death. The cries echo in my memory of those I've tried to comfort who were experiencing the pain of separation caused by death: "If I had only watched his diet more closely, he would still be alive." "If I had only taken her to the doctor earlier, she would not have suffered and died." "If I had only recognized the symptoms of severe depression, he would not have taken his own life."

Rejection, frequently a part of separation, causes pain. When a person divorces or abandons a mate, rejection is clear-cut. In one way or another, a person is told, "I don't like living with you. I don't want to be with you anymore. You are not lovable to me." Such attitudes, verbalized or not, hurt.

When a person becomes single because of a spouse's death, a sense of rejection may also be present. Strange as it may seem, the survivor may feel rejected by the dead mate. The attitude is something like this: "If he really loved me, he wouldn't have left me. He would have taken better care of himself. He would have managed to survive. He must not have wanted to be with me. There must be something wrong with me." Although such attitudes appear irrational, they are nonetheless real. People experiencing them need support, assurance, and encouragement.

Anger is a common emotion for those who are becoming single. In the case of divorce, husbands and wives are often—though not always—angry at each other. Blame, accusation, and insults may be hurled back and forth. Anger at a dying or dead mate is not at all uncommon. The feeling seems to be: "You wretch! How could you abandon me? How inconsiderate of you to leave me to cope alone." Anger at God is frequently felt but seldom expressed. "Why me?" is the question and charge leveled at God. The hidden meaning is, "I don't really deserve this. You're at fault for letting it happen to me. I'm angry with you." Often the most intense anger is reserved for oneself. There is a tendency in the throes of separation to blame oneself for what has happened. Self-anger carried on for an extended time is self-destructive, often leading to physical illness and even to death.

When we encounter someone who is angry as a result of separation, we can help by listening, allowing him to vent his feelings, and guiding him away from continuous nonproductive anger. Anger itself is a natural response to separation. A person should neither be shamed for expressing anger nor allowed to continue to wallow in it. Anger is but a phase; it must not be allowed to become a permanent aspect of life. The Bible guides us at this point: "Be ye angry and sin not: let not the sun go down upon your wrath" (Eph. 4:26). In other words, keep your anger in check, and don't keep it long.

Anxiety and fear usually plague those who go through the trauma of separation. These emotions are expressed in questions such as these: "How can life go on? What is to become of me? Will I ever be the same? Won't this happen again if I allow my life to become entangled with someone else's? Will I find someone else to relate to in a way that meets my needs?" Fear and anxiety can paralyze a person. An individual traumatized by separation often refuses to make decisions, draws away from interpersonal relationships, and is afraid to undertake even more simple tasks.

One of the best antidotes to anxiety and fear is assurance

from those who've been through similar experiences that life will go on and that the hurt will be eased. Some of the most effective ministry to those in the agony of separation is carried out by those who have suffered death of a loved one or who have been through a divorce. They are able to say, "I'm here to assure you that the bottom will hold. You don't think it will, but it will."

Suspicion and lack of trust often afflict those who are becoming single. They have been hurt, disappointed, and wounded. They don't want it to happen again. If a divorce involves infidelity, then there may be a reluctance to trust again. Promises have been broken, lies told, and trust mocked. As a result, the person who has been hurt pulls into a shell and shies away from involvement with others. One strategy to keep people from getting close is to hurt anyone who tries. Friends are often bewildered by this rejection. They need to understand the causes of such hostility and not take it personally. Wounded by divorce or death, a person lashes out, thrashes about in agony, and hurts others. The ministering Christian must absorb the blows and continue to care. What is needed is a tenacious caring, a bulldog type of hanging on.

Loneliness is one of the most difficult aspects of separation. The most intense loneliness often comes weeks and sometimes even months after a person becomes single. For a while there is the attention of those who care, the constant presence of concerned friends. Gradually, one by one, these drift back to the routine of their own daily life. Then the separated one is left alone. The nights grow longer and lonelier. During the day there is no one with whom to share deep feelings or experiences. Problems once discussed with another now must be faced alone. Fears once shared with another now must be dealt with alone. How important it is to see that there are persons available to whom the one who has suffered separation can relate.

Other problems plague the person who becomes single,

although they are not common to all: how to deal with sexuality, sexual desire, and the need for physical contact, cuddling, and stroking; how to cope with the difficulties of being a parent without a partner; how to deal with the pressures to conform—either to marry again quickly in a marriage-dominated society or to fit into the pattern of the swinging single.

Adequate response to the agony of becoming single embraces almost all of the mighty themes of the Bible. Indeed, this is a time to claim the promise of God: "God is our refuge and strength, a very present help in trouble" (Ps. 46:1). It is comforting to know that Jesus experienced the trauma of separation and came through victorious. His piercing cry, "My God, my God, why hast thou forsaken me?" (Matt. 27:46), was followed by a statement of faith: "Father, into thy hands I commend my spirit" (Luke 23:46). In fact, the only basic cure for the agony of separation is to put one's life into the hands of our loving heavenly Father. It may sound simplistic and pietistic, but it is nonetheless true. Only God can adequately comfort the brokenhearted, wipe away all tears from our eyes, and plant hope in the midst of the ruins of shattered lives.

Jesus, who has walked the way of separation before us and experienced the hurt involved, is the one who says, "Be of good cheer; it is I; be not afraid" (Matt. 14:27). He is also the one who has promised to send the Comforter and who declared, "I will not leave you comfortless; I will come to you" (John 14:18). By drawing close to Christ, the one who is becoming single can find strength and comfort.

Another great theme of the Bible is forgiveness. In many cases, separation comes because a person has sinned, been at fault, or fallen short of God's purpose. In such an instance, the path of hope leads through the gate of forgiveness. "If we confess our sins, he is faithful and just to forgive us our sins" (1 John 1:9). When we accept God's forgiveness and then forgive ourselves, we are equipped to march into the future with a sense of wholeness and confidence. Without that, the person who is becoming single is likely to continue to walk in guilt, self-pity, and anger.

Perhaps the most comforting word from the Bible in a period of separation concerns the love of God. Romans 8:31–39 indicates that although we may be separated from loved ones, we can never be separated from the love of our heavenly Father. Therefore, we are never really alone. Further, because of his presence and his love "we are more than conquerors" (v. 37); nothing can overcome us.

In addition to the promises from God's Word, the fellowship of believers, the family of God, offers help for those who are becoming single. This is no time to pull away from church involvement. When you go through the valley of separation, the journey is made bearable by being a part of God's family. Concerned Christian friends can provide relation during the hurt of separation. Whether it's a strong single adult program in a church or a small Sunday School class, a group of persons to whom an individual crippled by separation can relate is essential. Further, by participating in the broader community of Christian singles, a person begins to understand that singles enjoy significant purpose, possess gifts to share, can render service to others, and experience joy in Christ.

All formerly marrieds are by no means emotionally crippled. Many are doing quite well, thank you. In fact, they are coping with life better than numbers of persons who are married. They have a positive, healthy outlook. Those for whom the blow of separation has been crippling need contact with these who have life together in Christ. Even more important, they need relationship with Christ.

Jesus is one who teaches that the agony of separation is healed only by the miracle of relation. When the cry of separation "Why have you forsaken me?" is followed by the word of relation "Father, into your hands I commend my life," there is hope. That is the way of Jesus. And he bids us, "Follow me!"

Part 2: Special Days and Special Times

8

Giving Birth to a Baby Doesn't Make You a Mother
(Mother's Day)

When I call to remembrance the unfeigned faith that is in thee, which dwelt first in thy grandmother Lois, and thy mother Eunice; and I am persuaded that in thee also (2 Tim. 1:5).

For of this sort are they which creep into houses, and lead captive silly women laden with sins, led away with divers lusts,

Ever learning, and never able to come to the knowledge of the truth (2 Tim. 3:6–7).

The aged women likewise, that they be in behaviour as becometh holiness, not false accusers, not given to much wine, teachers of good things; that they may teach the young women to be sober, to love their husbands, to love their children (Titus 2:3–4).

In light of all the poetry and sentimental prose written about motherhood, it is surprising how little there is in the Bible about mothers or about motherhood as such. There's a reason for that, and it cuts across the grain of contemporary concepts about motherhood. At the risk of being stoned, I want to challenge those who worship in the cult of motherhood and set forth the Bible's teachings.

First, let me assure you that I really do like mothers. I've had the privilege of being closely related to several wonderful mothers. My two grandmothers were saintly. One of my grandmothers spent her last years dying of cancer in agony, often in bed, unable to get up. She, a Methodist, died joking with the Baptist preacher who had come to visit her. Her faith was so great that she could laugh in the face of death and pain.

My other grandmother died in her eighties, having gone to a meeting at her church, written her check to the Annie Armstrong Offering for missions, and prepared her own meal. Killed by a heart attack, she died with a smile on her face, knowing that her life had been lived fully and well. My early memories of visits to her home include going to church with her, praying with her, and being part of a happy household.

My own mother has again and again demonstrated Christian character. After surgery was performed on my father, she was busy scribbling notes to the first graders in her Sunday School class to tell them how much she missed being with them. My mother-in-law is one of the chief reasons I wanted to marry Bobbie. You don't marry a person; you marry a family. I wanted to be part of her mother's family. Not only is she a good cook, but she's a lot of fun. Bobbie is a wife and mother second to none. I love her and am proud of her.

You see, I really don't have anything against mothers. I've had good experiences with them. But I do think we have romanticized and idealized motherhood to the point that it is doing harm to mothers and children alike. Therefore, it's important to find out what the Bible says about mothering and what God wants in regard to children and mothers.

First, giving birth to a baby does not make a woman a mother. The Bible is quite realistic about this. The inspired writers of the New Testament lived in a world in which many children were born to women who did not want to keep them. Infant abandonment was common. Babies were left on garbage heaps, in the streets, and by the side of roads. They were often picked up by owners of brothels and trained to be prostitutes. They were sold into slavery. It was a horrible circumstance. The Bible doesn't propagate the sentimental idea that just because a person experiences the biological act of giving birth to a baby, she is automatically a mother.

Many women who have never given birth to a baby have been wonderful mothers. On the other hand, many women have experienced biological birth several times but have never really been mothers. Some give the baby to others to raise because they love their baby and, realizing there is no way for the child to be properly cared for, place it for adoption, in a foster home, or with in-laws or relatives. Some keep the child but never really become mothers. They treat the child as a thing—a toy to be played with, a doll to be dressed, a tool to be used in manipulating a husband, a weapon to gain benefits.

Motherhood is not basically a biological act or a physical relationship. It is a commitment. It is assuming responsibility to help develop the life of a child. It's getting your life all tangled up with children—hurting with them, laughing with them, crying with them, and living with them in good times and bad. In marriage a wife commits herself to her husband for better or for worse, for richer and poorer, in sickness and in health. But the commitment of a woman to a child in mothering is just as binding and lasting. Giving birth to a baby does not make you a mother; there is more to it than that.

Second, accepting responsibility to help a little life mature and grow does not automatically make a person good. The way some people talk, simply becoming a mother is qualification enough for sainthood. The fact is that many mothers are far from being saints. This was true in New Testament times. In 2 Timothy 3:6–7 the Bible speaks about women who were carried away by many kinds of false doctrine. In 1 Timothy 5:11–13 and Titus 2:3–5 the Bible describes women who went from house to house spending their time in gossip and slander. These women were mothers, but they were not good people.

The Bible teaches that the only way anyone becomes good is through experiencing the new birth, not by giving birth. A woman can give birth to a dozen children, but this biological exercise will not even inch her toward heaven. A woman can work at raising children until her body aches, read to them until her eyes blur, and answer their questions until her mind swims, but this will not put her name in the book of life. The only way a person is born again is by becoming a believer in Jesus Christ, not by giving birth to a baby. Let's be done with the sentimental heresy that mothers are saints simply because they are mothers and come to the biblical idea that righteousness comes only through repentance and faith—and that includes mothers.

It's hard for those who've been raised by a mother who cared for them, kissed away their hurts, put Mercurochrome on their skinned knees, and helped them with their homework to think of Mother as being lost, but she is lost unless she has trusted in Jesus Christ as her personal Lord and Savior. Doing good things for your children—or for anyone else—will not bring salvation. There is no substitute for the new birth. Frankly, I can't imagine a woman trying to be a mother without being a Christian. It's such an awesome responsibility; why would one dare try it alone when God stands ready to help, give his Spirit, guide, and encourage? If for no other reason, a woman ought to want to be a part of the family of God in order to obtain what God has to offer in helping with the heavy responsibility of mothering.

Third, becoming a Christian does not make a woman a skilled mother. You don't become a skilled anything by becoming a Christian. Yet the idea persists that by becoming a Christian, you automatically acquire certain skills. That's not the way salvation usually works—a new attitude, yes; new skills, no. What would you think of the following conversation with a friend who heard you complaining of a pain in your stomach?

"You know, I think if we did exploratory surgery we could find out what's wrong. Why don't you come by my house tomorrow and we'll open you up?"

"I didn't think you were a doctor."

"Oh, I'm not, but I got saved in a revival three weeks ago."

"Well, what's that got to do with opening me up?"

"Well, I mean, after all, I'm a Christian."

"That's great, but what skills of surgery come with being a Christian?"

"Well, I'm not sure. But I really care about you and want to help you."

Or imagine that someone hears your car clanking. This conversation takes place:

"Hey, why don't you bring your car by my house and I'll take that motor apart and find out what's wrong?"

"I didn't know you were a mechanic."

"I'm not, but I've driven cars for years; and recently I've become a Christian."

"What makes you think you can fix my car?"

"Well, I've been around cars all my life; I want to help you; and I just believe I can."

Sounds silly, doesn't it? But I've heard a person say about a woman, "Now that she's a Christian, what a wonderful mother she will make!" Nonsense. Becoming or being a Christian has little to do with the skills of motherhood. Why do you think Paul wrote to Titus and said, "Let those older women who have acquired the skills of mothering teach the younger ones to love their husbands and love their children"? I once thought anybody who became a mother instinctively knew how to care for the child; but experience and Bible study have taught me differently. Giving birth to a baby does not mean a woman automatically knows how to raise a child anymore than saying "I do" in a marriage ceremony means she knows how to be a good wife to a husband.

Effective mothering requires learning skills just as any serious responsibility calls for learning skills. And how many there are—teaching, nursing, organizing, nurturing, cooking, sanitizing, financing, playing, worshiping, comforting, motivating, disciplining, and scores of others! The skills do not automatically come with conversion. They are not special gifts from God bestowed without discipline or work. The skills of mothering are learned the way any skills are learned—through observation, education, practice, and discipline.

Fourth, even a skilled Christian mother will be less than perfect and will make many mistakes. After you've worked at the task, there's no assurance that you're going to be a perfect mother. In fact, you won't be. The Bible makes quite clear that all of us, including mothers, are sinful, less than perfect. Further, we are all, including mothers, limited in our knowledge. We are finite. We don't know everything. Therefore, all mothers sin; and they make many mistakes because of ignorance, lack of experience, and other inadequacies.

Christian mothers do have an edge on the non-Christians, to be sure. They know more about love because they have experienced God's love. They have the Bible to guide them in parenting. They enjoy fellowship in a church with older men and women who can share wisdom gained from experience and careful Bible study. Christian mothers know the value of family worship, of teaching children the Bible, of leading them to know Christ, of nurturing their faith. The finest thing a mother can share with her children is a knowledge and love of God.

A mother's faith is not a substitute for her child's own personal faith in Christ; no one can believe for another. There is no salvation by proxy. But a mother can help develop in her children an awareness of God's greatness and goodness. That's what Timothy's mother did for him: "When I call to remembrance the unfeigned faith that is in thee, which dwelt first in thy grandmother Lois, and thy mother Eunice" (2 Timothy 1:5).

Every child ought to have memories of prayer and worship times with Mother. Worship is more atmosphere and attitude than activity. Worship ought to be something all the family participates in. It's a sense of the presence of God. It's not being embarrassed at the name of Jesus. It's being quite confident that he is part of everything we do as a family. Worship is declaring the worth-ship of God for the best our family has to offer him. That means that work is worship and that play can be a kind of worship. There is also formal worship as a family reads the Bible together and prays. Families that worship together grow together in a kind of unity that is wonderful to behold.

Christian mothers have other resources at their disposal. They ought to be aware of the reality of sin and thus the importance of supervision, discipline, and forgiveness. They have access to power from the presence of the living Lord on which they can depend. They should see themselves for what they are—sinners prone to fall short of God's ideal, finite human beings liable to make mistakes. That's important because the high pedestal on which society has placed mothers is an uncomfortable perch.

Some continue to sanctify motherhood, pretending that mothers don't make mistakes if they really love their children and are Christians. This attitude can cause guilt and despair in women. The Christian mother should declare, "I am a sinner. I am limited in what I know. I will make mistakes in what I do. I am not perfect. God accepts me and loves me for what I am—and I hope you will too." Such an attitude has some pretty strong implications. For one thing, it means that children need to accept mothers as people, as human beings given to failures, faults, sins, and shortcomings. Mothers get angry. They can be selfish, greedy, gripy, moody, unfair, and harsh. They're not always easy to live with. They're not perfect. It's oppressive to have people continue to talk about how good you are when you know you are not. Let's take that load off of the mothers.

Some people grow to adulthood with a deep anger against their mother, a feeling that their mother let them down or failed them. But they are not able to express it. Our mother-worshiping culture frowns on talking about how a mother failed or what she did wrong. "Honor your father and mother" doesn't mean to be blind to the reality of sin in a mother's life.

One of my friends, a physician, had his life go from bad to worse; he lost his practice, became an alcoholic, suffered a divorce, hurt his children, and ruined their lives. Finally, in desperation, he attended a prayer retreat. God ministered to him; he realized he had been hating his mother most of his life but was unwilling to admit it. Like a dam bursting, the tears came as he wept and wept. In that moment he forgave her and accepted her. Then his life began to be put back together again. Don't blame a mother for your difficulties; accept your responsibility for your life and her nature as a human being in need of forgiveness.

A mother needs to accept herself as a finite, sinful human being and not allow herself to be crammed into the mold the world has shaped for her. She is not supermother, able to leap tall buildings in a single bound or to solve all the problems of her family. She is a mere human being. Carrying the load she does, she will make many mistakes—some of them quite serious, some to the permanent harm of her children. She needs to accept the promise of God that he does indeed forgive. He makes every day new. But to receive God's gift of new life we must come to him, confess our sin, and allow him to begin to build into us a better us for tomorrow.

Some mothers are trapped by guilt; they despair because they feel they've failed in their task. In some cases the sense of failure results from the too-high expectations set for them. In others it occurs because they have made mistakes in the past that may not be rectifiable in the present. That's why we need to invite God into our lives with his power and his forgiveness. He has the ability to wipe away tears, to heal hurt, and to say, "Do what you can. Accept who you are. Depend on my love and grace." If you're able to do that, you'll be able to relate to mothering in a way you never dreamed possible.

God's grace and forgiveness do not provide an excuse for failing to do the best job possible as a mother. Every mother has a responsibility to develop her life in order to be helpful to her children and to learn the skills of mothering. Yet it is important to remember that a mother's best will not be perfect and that grace and forgiveness must be part of her experience or she will live in perpetual despair. That's not what God intends. He wants you to have life abundant. It's yours in Christ.

9

When Fathers Fail
(Father's Day)

And the king was much moved, and went up to the chamber over the gate, and wept: and as he went, thus he said, O my son Absalom, my son, my son Absalom! would God I had died for thee, O Absalom, my son, my son! (2 Sam. 18:33).

The bad parenthood of good people is nothing new. The Old Testament contains a failure story about family life involving a man who succeeded in most other dimensions of life. He succeeded in politics. He succeeded as a poet. He succeeded as a theologian. He succeeded as a priestly type of man who led his nation to God. He succeeded as a writer. He succeeded as a military leader. The Bible says he was a man after God's own heart. But when it came to family, King David fell short. He failed as a father. Incest, adultery, murder, and rebellion—David's children were guilty of them all.

Absalom, his son, led a revolt against his father, trying to unseat him as the king of Israel. The king instructed his generals not to harm Absalom, but in the battle David's generals did not follow these orders. Absalom, riding a mule, was caught by the hair in a tree. The mule ran out from under him, leaving him dangling, a rather undignified situation for a rebel leader. He could not free himself or defend himself. He was hanging helpless in the tree when one of David's men threw darts into the heart of Absalom and killed him. Two messengers were sent to David with news about the battle. One went before the death of Absalom and the second afterward. The Bible says:

And David sat between the two gates: and the watchman went up to the roof over the gate unto the wall, and lifted up his eyes, and looked, and behold a man running alone.

And the watchman cried, and told the king. And the king said, If he be alone, there is tidings in his mouth. And he came apace, and drew near.

And the watchman saw another man running: and the watchman called unto the porter, and said, Behold another man running alone. And the king said, He also bringeth tidings.

And the watchman said, Me thinketh the running of the foremost is like the running of Ahimaaz the son of Zadok. And the king said, He is a good man, and cometh with good tidings.

And Ahimaaz called, and said unto the king, All is well. And he fell down to the earth upon his face before the king, and said, Blessed be the Lord thy God, which hath delivered up the men that lifted up their hand against my lord the king.

And the king said, Is the young man Absalom safe? And Ahimaaz answered, When Joab sent the king's servant, and me thy servant, I saw a great tumult, but I knew not what it was.

And the king said unto him, Turn aside, and stand here. And he turned aside, and stood still.

And, behold, Cushi came; and Cushi said, Tidings, my lord the king: for the Lord hath avenged thee this day of all them that rose against thee.

And the king said unto Cushi, Is the young man Absalom safe? And Cushi answered, The enemies of my lord the king, and all that rise against thee to do thee hurt, be as that young man is.

And the king was much moved, and went up to the chamber over the gate, and wept: and as he went, thus he said, O my son Absalom, my son, my son Absalom! would God I had died for thee, O Absalom, my son, my son! (2 Sam. 18:24–33).

When a father fails it hurts. David's failure cost Absalom and many other men their lives and cost David a broken heart. If David failed, any father can fail. No one is immune. Certainly David was not perfect. Gross sin scarred his life. Yet he was a great man, wise and devout. How could such a man fail as a father? The Bible doesn't say. It's necessary to explore David's entire life to get the picture.

Of course, the whole blame doesn't rest with David. Many other persons influenced Absalom's life. Further, Absalom was responsible for his own life. He was an adult. He didn't have to rebel. We are responsible for our actions, the Bible teaches, regardless of the kind of parents we have. It's interesting that people who are successful often claim to be self-made, while those who fail often blame their parents, environment, society, or schools. The Bible teaches that we are responsible persons, free to choose right or wrong. If we were totally conditioned by heredity or environment, we would be without freedom. Without freedom there would be no responsibility, no need to talk about standards, no need to discuss decision making.

Because a child grows up to be a destructive adult doesn't mean we should point an accusing finger at the parents and say, "You did something wrong or your child would have turned out all right." It is possible for parents to do just about everything right and for a child to turn out badly. Parents aren't the only ones who shape a child. Practically everyone with whom the child comes in contact has an influence—Sunday School teachers, Church Training leaders, choir directors, schoolteachers, relatives, neighbors, peers, friends, classmates. A child is also affected by input from the media, his environment, and various events he observes. Certain experiences may have an impact out of proportion to their apparent importance. Parents have little or no control over much of this. A child may grow up in a fine family with godly parents, who try hard and seemingly do all of the right things, and still be rebellious and destructive.

The fault was not all David's. Others influenced Absalom's life. Absalom was responsible too. Yet a parent does help shape the character and personality of children. And so many of David's offspring were failures that it is clear that he performed poorly as a parent. What did David do as a parent that was wrong?

David doted on Absalom and did not discipline him. David played favorites with his children. He gave Absalom more attention than the others, even though Absalom seems to have been persistently a rebellious person who regarded his father with a venomous attitude. Nevertheless, Absalom continued to be David's pet. This doting undercut discipline so that when Absalom did something wrong, rather than disciplining him, David knuckled under. Was he afraid of Absalom? afraid of being rejected by Absalom? afraid of what Absalom might do to him in his old age? Many otherwise brave men seem to fear their children. Whatever the reason, David simply would not discipline his son. As Absalom grew up under this doting parent who refused to discipline, he became more and more corrupt.

It is the same with parent-child relations today. The parent who dotes and doesn't discipline damages the child. Real love leads to discipline. Parents back away from effective discipline for many reasons. A child born to an older couple may get more the grandparent than the parent treatment. A child who is handicapped or who is suffering from a disease may be coddled, enveloped in an overprotective atmosphere. Some parents play favorites. Others seem to fear a child. For whatever reasons, without consistent discipline, a child has little opportunity to develop in the way he should. Only when we have resistance do we grow strong. We don't develop muscles by lifting a feather; we develop by pushing or lifting things that create resistance. Discipline is a means of resistance within a family to strengthen character. It is also a means of guiding people, of leading them from destructive to constructive activity.

The major reason for lack of discipline, I believe, is the difficulty of the task. Discipline is usually resisted. Few children prefer discipline to ice cream. It is easier to say "Well, if you want to, that's all right" than "No, you may not do that." When a child is told no and continues to badger and beg, the course of least resistance is to give in and say, "Don't bother me; go ahead and do it." Many parents have sighed, "Well, I guess it will be all right this time" when they really didn't feel it would be all right at all. Weary of the struggle, they give in. Sometimes parents are afraid to say no because they fear that their child will be ostracized, made fun of, if he doesn't go along with the crowd. When many other parents are saying "It's OK," saying no becomes even more difficult. But parents need to stand firm by their convictions and not be controlled by other families or manipulated by their own children. Certainly they shouldn't abort discipline because it's difficult.

Discipline is not child abuse. It is whatever works to turn a child away from harmful habits, attitudes, and practices. It is consistent guidance with a loving no placed against a child's life to help mold him in God's pattern. It is administering punishment that is just, that does not nag or needlessly provoke a child to wrath. It is the willingness to take the guff that comes from one who is being resisted and let him known of love and concern.

The unhappiest persons are those who have grown up either with cruel and unjust punishment or with no discipline at all. During a church youth retreat one weekend with about a hundred high school students, I noticed three tough-looking characters hanging around the fringes wearing cynical snarls. They stood apart, almost aloof, with a smugness that comes from pseudosophistication.

During a sharing time the students began to tell what they appreciated about their parents. One girl said, "Although I guess I'd never admit it to my folks, I appreciate the fact they have rules for me and expect me to live by them. For example, I have to be in at a certain time. I don't always like it, but it makes me feel good to know they love me enough to care what I do and where I go. And I feel secure knowing they'll stand firm, even though I gripe." Several others said essentially the same thing.

I noticed the three men of the world sniffing back tears.

Puzzled, I later asked about them and learned they came from families who said, "Go ahead and do what you want. Don't bother us." They realized that they were missing something—parents who loved enough to discipline. Discipline, rightly administered, might have saved Absalom from destruction. But David, the doting father, allowed his son to grow as a wild weed with no cultivation at all.

Second, David gave his son every thing but evidently gave little of himself. Absalom had the finest clothes. He had choice living quarters. He enjoyed prosperity—chariots, horses, servants to do his bidding. Whenever he wanted anything, all he had to do was say, "Dad, can I have it?" And David would say, "Sure. After all, you are the king's son. You are my favorite." But when Absalom wanted time with his father, he heard, "Sorry, son, but I'm busy. Maybe next week. Here's some money. Go have a good time."

A void developed in Absalom. He began to wonder if his father was trying to buy his affection. David gave things rather than himself. The person who is constantly given things but never given love, companionship, and affection begins to be rebellious. The rebellion is a way of saying, "Don't give me any *thing* else. Give me yourself. Relate to me. Notice me. Argue with me. Love me. Affirm me. Do something with me. Don't just lay another thing into my life." The only time David paid attention to Absalom was when his son was rebellious. Then he would relate to him, but soon would move back into the pattern of ignoring him. Of course, that only stimulated Absalom's rebellion—a way of both getting his father's attention and punishing him for his lack of attention.

Do you know any parents and children with a David-Absalom relationship? I do. Many of them. Such parents don't purposely ignore their children, but they spend little creative time with them. Somehow they think there will always be opportunity to be with their children, so they concentrate on business, civic activity, social affairs, or church life. In the end such benign neglect bears horrible dividends.

The opportunity to be with children is brief. They quickly grow up. The direction of their life is fashioned early and cannot be easily changed. Often I visit with persons whose children are in serious difficulty; they wring their hands and cry, "What can I do to correct this?" I know that outside of a miracle there isn't anything that can be done to correct it. The situation has gone too far. The parents' opportunity is past. You can't stop a landslide after you've set off the dynamite and after tons of rock and dirt are tumbling down the mountain. It's too late. David's pathetic cry echoed over the surrounding hills: "O my son Absalom, my son, my son Absalom! would God I had died for thee, O Absalom, my son, my son!" What God wanted was not for David to die for Absalom but for David to live for him, relate to him, spend time with him, discipline him, parent him. But David didn't do these things. What a price he paid for his neglect.

How should a father respond to failure? David wept and wept and wept. In fact, he grieved so deeply that his people finally had to come and say: "You can't go on like this. It is bad for your health and the morale of the nation. You mustn't continue to weep over this dead son who was a rebel. You must remember that you have responsibility for your people, for the rest of your family, for yourself." David began to emerge from his time of mourning. I think he recognized that although Absalom's rebellion and death were largely the result of his failure as a father, God would forgive him and life would go on.

Handling failure as a parent is difficult. It seems to involve several basic ingredients. First, there is acceptance of the fact that things have not gone well; there is no gain in pretending all is well when it isn't.

Second, responsibility for the failure must be accepted, and not in an overdramatic fashion ("It's all my fault!"). That usually isn't true at all. A realistic assessment of personal responsibility must be made.

Third, grief ought to come. We should be sorry; we ought to weep. Part of grief is mourning the hurt of a loved one, and part of it is mourning our own loss. Grief is natural. Sometimes it is rooted in selfishness—embarrassment over a child gone astray, anger at not being in control, feeling sorry for oneself. But nevertheless, it is part of being human and a necessary ingredient in working through loss, hurt, and failure.

Fourth, forgiveness must enter the picture. Failure ought to lead to confession of our sins to God, who is the only one who can forgive. Failure as a parent is a sin. Like any other sin, it calls for confession, repentance, and acceptance of God's forgiveness.

Fifth, the task of daily life should be resumed. There is work to be done, family members to be loved, and experiences to be enjoyed after even the most terrible of catastrophes.

David followed these basic steps. To his credit, although he failed as a father, he did not let that failure continue to wreck his life. Instead, he pulled himself together, accepted Absalom's death, realized his responsibility, grieved, and went back to work. He began to govern his people, to do the task that was his. David was a man after God's own heart; he knew that if he confessed his sin to God, God would cleanse him, restore him to fellowship, and help him move on through life. People don't expect you to mourn forever.

But you say, "You just don't understand. What I've done is horrible. I feel so guilty about having failed. And it's so embarrassing because people know." Few have failed as thoroughly as David failed. His son attempted to overthrow a government, kill his father, and destroy a multitude of people. His son's activities were known to everyone. Speak about public humiliation, embarrassment, guilt, failure in a terrible way—David knew about them all. But he also knew a Father who had a rebellious child whose name was David, a child who had sinned grossly but had been forgiven. Knowing that Father, David could go to him, lean on him, confess to him, accept his forgiveness, and continue to live. That's what we ought to do. It's important to try not to fail, to avoid the mistake David made. It is also important to know what to do when you fail because you will—all of us will in some way. And when you do, the response should not be perpetual weeping. Rather, it ought to be confession, repentance, forgiveness, and life.

That is what the gospel is about—how God provided for our failures through Jesus. Jesus died on a cross for sinners, for failures such as we are. When we fail we can shrug and pretend we don't really care. Or we can face the catastrophe with stoic acceptance. Or we can wallow in excessive, extensive grief. But there is a better way. It comes through him who said, "I am the way, the truth, and the life. No man cometh to the Father, but by me" (John 14:6). By faith come to the Father by Jesus. He makes life new every morning. When you fail and your heart is broken, he understands. When you confess, he forgives. When you reach out for hope in the dark night of despair, he is there.

10

Christian Discipleship and Family Life
(Revival)

Hear therefore, O Israel, and observe to do it; that it may be well with thee, and that ye may increase mightily, as the Lord God of thy fathers hath promised thee, in the land that floweth with milk and honey.

Hear, O Israel: The Lord our God is one Lord:

And thou shalt love the Lord thy God with all thine heart, and with all thy soul, and with all thy might.

And these words, which I command thee this day, shall be in thine heart:

And thou shalt teach them diligently unto thy children, and shall talk of them when thou sittest in thine house, and when thou walkest by the way, and when thou liest down, and when thou risest up.

And thou shalt bind them for a sign upon thine hand, and they shall be as frontlets between thine eyes.

And thou shalt write them upon the posts of thy house, and on thy gates.

And it shall be, when the Lord thy God shall have brought thee into the land which he sware unto thy fathers, to Abraham, to Isaac, and to Jacob, to give thee great and goodly cities, which thou buildest not,

And houses full of all good things, which thou filledst not, and wells digged, which thou diggedst not, vineyards and olive trees, which thou plantedst not; when thou shalt have eaten and be full;

Then beware lest thou forget the Lord, which brought thee forth out of the land of Egypt, from the house of bondage (Deut. 6:3-12).

Before the people who followed Jesus were labeled Christians, they were called disciples. Before they were known as believers, they were referred to as disciples. In fact, in the New Testament *disciple* is one of the first and most frequently used words for the followers of Jesus.

Discipleship is basic in the Christian walk. It means learning about and following after Jesus Christ in all aspects of life—in our personal attitudes, witness, church, family, community, work, leisure, and government. No area of life should be shut off from discipleship. That's why Jesus talked to his followers about family and politics, why he discussed daily work and witness, why he walked with them through all of life's experiences. He shared with them—and us—that Christian discipleship is to touch everything we are and everything that we'll ever be.

One important area of discipleship is family. A person cannot be a good Christian unless he is a good family member. No one can be all that God wants unless his family life is Christ-saturated. Husbands, wives, parents, children, in-laws, and relatives all have a responsibility to express Christian discipleship through family life.

In the sixth chapter of Deuteronomy, God set forth for his people how they were to relate family life to his word, how parents and children were to be disciples. The instructions are not out of date. True, they were given to the people of Israel as they went into the Promised Land; but these words also apply to us, the disciples of Jesus Christ. The New Testament emphasizes family life. Matthew 5 and 19, 1 Corinthians 7, Ephesians 5—6, and Colossians 3 contain special sections on family. In almost every part of the Bible God speaks to us from his Word about our families. No one who takes the Bible seriously can take family life lightly.

According to the Bible, discipleship is to be expressed through family members helping one another to grow spiritually, learning about God's Word and about his ways. Deuteronomy 6 commands the people to learn about God within the family setting. As recorded in Deuteronomy, when a person gets up in the morning he is to read the Scriptures or recite them from memory. As he goes about his work during the day he is to recall verses of Scripture. The Word of God is to be a constant daily companion.

Because the Word of God was to be a central feature in a Jewish family, Scriptures were visible at all times. Portions of Scripture were written on the doorposts or on little bits of parchment worn around wrists or on the head. Later some Jews reduced those practices to mere ritual. They kept the letter of the command but forgot to fulfill its purpose. They wrote Scriptures on the doorposts and wore Scriptures around their wrists and heads, but they didn't put God's Word in their hearts. It's not enough to have the Bible visible—on a table, a shelf, or a desk. We are also to read, ponder, and make it part of our lives.

Day after day a family is to read the Bible, share the Bible, study the Bible, memorize the Bible, and quote the Bible so that it becomes part of life and not an appendage to it. That's not easy to do in a busy family's schedule, but it can be done. The Bible ought to be read at the beginning and the end of each day. It ought to be part of those moments in which families are together before going into the frantic activity of the workaday world and after coming home.

Does your family make the Bible a consistent part of daily life? Do you begin and end the day with the Scriptures? Do the members of your family carry the Word of God in their minds and hearts so they can utilize it as crises come? With tragic consequences we let almost anything come in the way of daily family time with the Word of God.

Parents are primarily responsible for the spiritual welfare of the family. The Bible says, "Thou shalt teach them diligently unto thy children." Children have a responsibility, however, to say to parents, "When will we study the Scriptures? When will we read the Bible? When will we memorize the Word of God?" Parents and youth working together like the pedals on a bicycle can keep things moving along God's way. Is it that way in your house?

In our family we've found that the style or method ought to vary according to the age of children, schedule, and location. When we are visiting in someone's home we usually share in what that family does, for example. Generally we have discovered that a routine at breakfast works well for us. Each member of our family is responsible for a week of Bible study and devotion at a time. I often use maps and objects to teach about biblical persons and events. Bobbie majors on Scripture memory with us. Meredith usually reads a portion of Scripture, frequently from the Psalms, and directs a prayer time. Allison often uses her Sunday School lesson as a guide. Night is usually a time for individual Bible reading or sometimes sharing one-to-one. Although we are not as consistent as I'd like, my personal testimony is that family life functions much much better when a family time with God's Word begins and ends the day.

The Bible teaches that discipleship is to be expressed through family life by worship. In both the Old Testament and the New Testament, worship was primarily a family affair. When the people of Israel were led by God from slavery into the Promised Land there were no temples, no synagogues, and few places for religious meetings. The main way people learned about God was through the family. One reason why Jewish families today are some of the most stable in society may be because religious education among Jews has centered in family life. Faith and family have been linked together. Religious devotion strengthened family life, and families contributed to religious fervor.

After the Temple was built, families came to worship in it on special religious occasions. When synagogues became part of the Jewish religious scene, people gathered in them on the sabbath for worship and study of the Scriptures. The

New Testament indicates that the first Christians were Jews, many of whom continued to worship in the Temple and meet in synagogues. As Christians became more aware of their distinctiveness, they met in homes for fellowship, worship, and study. Later they began to congregate in special buildings. Still, the family remained the center of worship and religious instruction.

Worship practices in churches have changed through the centuries, but worship by families has remained much the same. Informal family worship usually includes reading the Bible, praying, expressing needs, remembering absent members, and singing. Sometimes family worship is more formal with candles, devotionals, and special music.

Whether formal or informal, the event centers in expressing the "worthship" of God for the devotion of the entire family. Worship means just that—worthship, that God is worth everything we are and have. Worship is expressed by how a family uses its talents and possessions. If we spend more for personal luxuries than for extending the gospel, the message is clear: We care more about things than we do about God. If more is spent on frivolous items than on sending missionaries around the world to preach the gospel, our talk about how much we love God comes through to others as shallow and hypocritical. Worship is expressed in daily family life by relating to one another in Christian love, by being fair and thoughtful, by showing that God is alive and well in family routine. Worship should never be a dull, boring experience. Rather, it is to be a discovery of how wonderful God is. Worship is sharing the miracles that God performs in life, the prayers that he answers, the joy that he gives.

Has your family disciplined itself for a regular time of worship? Do you have a certain place for worship? What plan do you use? Do you vary the procedure to avoid the dullness of routine? Is worship a show parents put on for children, or do adults maintain worship when children are not present? How do you utilize the Bible in worship? other devotional material? What contribution does each family member make? How do you overcome the problem of busyness, fractured family life, and conflicting time schedules? Family worship calls for careful planning, dedication, and effort—but it's worth it.

Some of the happiest times we have had as a family center in family worship. Apart from the prayer and share time in conjunction with morning and evening Bible reading, we don't make a big production of family worship every day. Special worship times are part of family life. Frequently our two daughters have planned and conducted the family worship, including special music, skits, and devotionals. We have used music, filmstrips, and slides to add variety. Holidays afford times for special family worship. For example, at Christmas we set up seven candles as part of our manger scene. Each night the week before Christmas we light a candle, read a Bible passage related to Christ's birth, pray, and open presents from our family who are scattered throughout the United States. Christmas Day begins with a similar worship time before we "have the tree." Special worship traditions are also important in our family for Easter, birthdays, and Thanksgiving.

Discipleship is to be expressed in family life through ministry and service. The people of Israel, as they moved into the Promised Land, were given special commandments about care for strangers, the poor, orphans, and widows. Each family unit was primarily responsible for seeing that its members did not suffer want and that strangers who came through the land were cared for.

In the New Testament the emphasis on care for the poor and powerless continued. Jesus criticized those who did not provide for their aging parents (Matt. 15:3-6). Church leaders declared that a person who did not provide for his own family was worse than an infidel (1 Tim. 5:8), that parents ought to provide for their children so that they would not be a burden on others (2 Cor. 12:14). Christian families were urged to share what they possessed with persons in need (2 Cor. 8:7-15). Babies were rescued from garbage heaps where they had been dumped by pagan Romans. Widows were placed on special rolls to be supported by Christian families (1 Tim. 5:3-16).

Such display of ministry and service did not go unnoticed in the pagan world. Pagans began to say about these Christian families, "There is something different about them. They care about one another. They stick together; but more than that, they reach out to help others in love and ministry." The non-Christians also noticed that the families of believers opposed practices that destroyed human life. They attacked social issues that reeked with injustice. In a sexually polluted society they took their stand for purity. In a world where slavery was cruel they dared declare that slaves were to be treated as brothers and sisters in Christ. They tore down walls that separated people into hostile camps. These families demonstrated that they were different.

A ministering kind of family life is needed today. Is it expressed in your family? What have you done recently for someone outside your family? Whom have you gone to see, written, taken gifts to, shared job opportunities with, brought into the fellowship when they were lonely and frightened? Have you helped the separated, divorced, and widowed feel the warmth of your own family setting? Do you work together as a family to right the wrongs in our world—hunger, racism, injustice, abuse of persons? Do you learn together about the problems in government, economics, education, and other areas and about what can be done about them? People who do something significant to turn the world right side up frequently catch the vision in a family setting.

The Bible also teaches that we should express discipleship through family life by evangelism. In the Old Testament sharing good news about God was not consistently done outside the family of faith. The Jewish people had difficulty believing that God really loved the whole world. When God called Jonah to preach to Nineveh, for example, at first the prophet didn't want to do it. But God continued to reveal that he was the God of all, not just the God of Israel. The prophets of the eighth century—Amos, Micah, Isaiah, and Hosea—clearly declared that God, Yahweh, was not the tribal god of a small band of desert wanderers. He was the God Creator, the God Sustainer, the God Redeemer of all people.

God called Israel to the task of being the channel of redemption to the world. When they resisted, the task of being evangels passed to us as Jesus' followers. We are to share the good news with everybody, to be the channel of redemption. In the early days of the Christian movement there were no church buildings, no highly organized congregations, no denominational agencies, no mission boards, no seminaries. The first Christians evangelized and ministered within two basic structures, local churches and family units.

Paul wrote about "the church in thy house," house churches. The churches were a sort of extended family with a father, or pastor, of the group. Other persons began to assume special responsibilities in that "family"—teachers, evangelists, proclaimers, ministers, and administrators—according to their gifts. Family units also played a big part in the Christian mission in those first years. Early church leaders realized that the family was the key to evangelism, Christian growth, and ministry. Timothy, one of the early Christian leaders, was evidently the product of home evangelism. Paul wrote to him, "When I call to remembrance the unfeigned faith that is in thee, which dwelt first in thy grandmother Lois, and thy mother Eunice, and I am persuaded that in thee also" (2 Tim. 1:5).

Evangelism in the future may also be done largely through families. Certainly the church will maintain a role of prominence. Revival meetings will continue to have a place. Visitation programs will reach certain people who will respond to the message of the gospel. But more and more, evangelism will be done through family units—families living in apartment house complexes, families in neighborhoods, families in mobile home parks, families in recreation centers. God will work through families.

Few unsaved people come to church meetings unless they are visited, invited, and prayed for. With apartment houses increasing, both husband and wife working, leisuretime and opportunities expanding, and children's activities accelerating, typical church visitation programs are becoming less and less effective. A family ministry approach is called for in which each family in Christ serves as a center for witness and ministry among other families nearby. Cells of Christlike compassion, these families can make a difference in a mobile home park, an apartment house, or a suburban neighborhood.

And what kind of families will God be able to use? Families with a prayer list of people who are lost. Families who pray by name for people about whom they are concerned. Families who care about young people, children, adults, and the aging. Families who share the Word of God freely. Familes who invite others to join them for Bible study. Families who share through example the joy of being in Christ Jesus.

Do you have that kind of family? Is your family an evangelistic unit—praying, reaching out, bringing in, visiting, expressing concern? Is the evidence of the gospel seen in your community, apartment house, or neighborhood because of your family?

The discipleship of the people of God is expressed in our families through Christian nurture, worship, ministry, and evangelism. I wonder if I've described your family. If I haven't, would you talk to God about helping you to make it conform to his way? And will you pray for others that each family of Christians will be truly a family of God, a band of disciples?

11

Aging: A Christian Response
(Senior Adult Day)

Remember the days of old, consider the years of many generations: ask thy father, and he will shew thee; thy elders, and they will tell thee (Deut. 32:7).

Hearken unto thy father that begat thee, and despise not thy mother when she is old (Prov. 23:22).

"Old Man Hunt"—that's what he was called in my hometown. I remember him vividly—blind, cane tapping as he shuffled from his one-room shack to the town square where he begged, dirty beard, old clothes. We kids would taunt him; he would yell and swing his cane wildly, and we'd laugh. What we did was bad. What the town and churches did was bad too. They ignored him. Near where Old Man Hunt begged, the "Spit and Whittle Domino Club" met; day after day a group of old men played dominoes, chewed tobacco, and whittled. My idea of old age formed in my hometown was terrible.

But there were other influences. Kindly old neighbors talked with me, cared for me, and took an interest in me. During much of my growing-up time my grandparents were active, enthusiastic people. A great-uncle took me fishing and hunting. A great-aunt, full of energy and interest, was always involved in a project, perpetually planning for the future. From these I learned a different concept of old age: good old age. Most people share my mixed impressions, I think, of good old age and terrible old age. But all of us agree that we Christians have a special responsibility for older persons.

Persons over sixty-five are no more all alike than those of

any age. Yet enough common characteristics exist to make it worthwhile to identify them. Too often old age is associated only with problems. The positive features are overlooked. As a result, the resources and abilities of the senior adults are neglected to everyone's loss. Older people cite numerous good points about their stage in life. Among the most common mentioned are these:

- Release from the pressures of a job.
- Freedom to begin a second career, concentrate on interests previously neglected, or travel.
- Time for more adequate health care.
- Choice of friends on the basis of congeniality, not job or other responsibilities.
- Opportunity for using skills and time in a more concentrated ministry to others.
- Better control of emotions with resulting serenity.
- Self-acceptance and lack of intense competition with others.

Not every senior adult enjoys these, of course. But the fact that many do indicates that old age can be looked upon not so much with dread but with hope.

To determine what response ought to be made to the senior adults, we must understand the nature of their needs and problems. Purpose and meaning for life heads the list of needs. In a materialistic, technological, work-oriented society a person's worth is often measured in terms of production, income, and possessions. Older persons often experience a sense of loss of purpose, meaning, and worth when they retire. They need to know that they are still important and needed, to experience a sense of belonging, to feel loved. Although most older adults are not neglected by their grown children in the sense of never being visited or contacted, they often feel unwanted, unloved, or useless.

Millions of older adults fill their days with meaningful activity—ministry to others, reading, adult education, hobbies, travel, gardening and yard care, work, and professional activity. But others sit and brood or watch endless hours of television, the activity that ranks first in the way senior adults spend their time. Feeling unloved, unwanted, and guilty about being nonproductive, many older persons slip into depression. As friends die and family members move away, loneliness may settle like a thick, dark cloud. Other problems compound the sense of frustration, and many just give up. Suicide and mental illness rates are high among the elderly, especially the men.

Health is a second big problem. Although many older persons over sixty-five enjoy good health—for some, better than when younger—most experience an increase in health-related problems. Fear of illness, with the high cost of medical care, is the number 1 concern of most senior adults. The facts bear out the fear. The majority of older Americans have one or more chronic health problems. Health problems are aggravated by several factors. Many older people fail to prepare or eat adequate meals. Sometimes there is not enough money to buy food for a balanced diet. The current inflationary spiral is especially hard on senior adults with fixed incomes.

Where to live is a major concern for many seniors. Most prefer to live in their own home and do. But many of these houses are dilapidated and in transitional areas with deteriorating neighborhoods, high crime rates, and increasing business activity. Unable to move because of the high cost of other housing, these older persons are sentenced to live out their days in substandard circumstances. Rising taxes, repair costs, and utility rates threaten many elderly persons with the loss of their home. Already senior citizens spend more on housing than any other item.

Household chores become more difficult as one grows older. Cleaning, washing clothes and dishes, preparing meals, repairing the house, and taking care of the yard may overwhelm the senior citizen. Some tasks become too dangerous to tackle, such as climbing ladders to replace light bulbs. Few can afford to hire persons to help with the housekeeping, maintenance, and repairs.

When they can no longer live in their own home, forced

to leave because of poor health or soaring housing costs, the options of where to go are often undesirable. Some institutions for the aging are quite comfortable, but usually expensive for a low-income budget. Others are depressing and even dangerous. Living with grown children is the route many take. Such an arrangement raises many issues. Open discussion among all members of the family, patience, and love are necessary ingredients for making such an arrangement satisfactory. Unfortunately, many families fall apart into squabbling camps over the decision of where aging parents are to live.

Transportation is another major problem. Older people become increasingly dependent on others for transportation. Poor eyesight and slowed reflexes may deprive them of the right to drive. Income may be inadequate to afford the high price of operating an automobile. Public transportation may be unavailable or inaccessible. Inadequate transportation accentuates the other problems of the elderly. Getting to the grocery store, doctor's office, church, post office, and other important places becomes a huge chore. As a result, many slight grocery buying, doctor's visits, church, and recreational activity.

The problems of aging often are made more difficult because of inadequate income. Low income makes it practically impossible for millions of older persons to have adequate health care, housing, or food.

Interpersonal relations are often a problem for the aging. For many, the older years are more placid than the earlier, family ties closer, and friendships more meaningful. But these years can also put a strain on relationships. Retirement is often a stressful time within a family unless careful planning and preparation have been made. "Too much husband, too little income" is the lament of many a wife when her mate retires. Competition for the affection of grown children, grandchildren, and friends can be a problem. Grief over the death of one's mate, friends, and family is a common experience for the elderly.

Dealing with death, something we all must do, is a problem

for the aging. Some fear death. Most fear the pain, expense, and inconvenience of taking a long time to die. More and more are demanding the right to a natural death with no medical heroics to prolong illness. The nearness of death calls for spiritual preparation in order to be ready to die well. It also means that wills and other legal matters should be attended to. Plans for the body must be made. But many people delay these matters, refusing to face the reality of death.

A church family cannot be content merely to describe and analyze the aging. We must act in response to human need. More and more churches are realizing the need for special programs related to the aging. Consequently, many churches now have one or more ministries with and to older persons. What we have done is only a beginning of what we should do. But what should we do? as a church? as families? as individuals? We will all have to work on the answer to that question. What I have to suggest is limited and is painted in broad, general strokes. The place to begin is *attitude*, how we feel and think about aging. If we are faithful to the teaching of the Bible, we will look upon aging positively.

Old age is viewed by the inspired writers of the Scripture as a blessing; "good old age" is the way the Bible puts it (Gen. 15:15; 25:8; Judg. 8:32; 1 Chron. 29:28; Job 42:17). Age is seen as an indication of God's favor (Deut. 4:40; 5:33; 11:19–21; 1 Kings 3:14; Job 5:26; Ps. 91:16; Prov. 3:1–2; Isa. 46:4). Old age is characterized by wisdom and integrity (Prov. 3:13–16; 9:10–11; 20:29). The Bible clearly teaches that the aged are to be treated with honor and respect (Lev. 19:32; Prov. 23:22; Job 32:4; 1 Tim. 5:1–2). The command "Honour thy father and thy mother" (Ex. 20:12) is an especially important injunction, as Paul pointed out (Eph. 6:2). Although it applies to all parents and children, it certainly relates to children with aged parents. The elderly are to be cared and provided for (1 Tim. 5:4,8). Not even religious devotion is to stand in the way of children's meeting the needs of their parents (Matt. 15:1–9).

The Bible also makes it clear that the aging have responsibilities to God and other persons. There is no such thing as retirement from Christian responsibility. The older members of the community are to be accorded a place of responsibility, as well as respect (Deut. 32:7). The Bible records how God worked through the lives of older persons obedient to his will. Abraham began a new adventure under God's direction when he was a senior adult; Sarah and Elizabeth gave birth to children important to God's plans when they were old; Moses was eighty when God called him to lead his people out of Egypt; David still reigned as king when he was elderly; John wrote some of the most meaningful portions of the New Testament when he was old. The Bible teaches that "good old age" and faithfulness to God are related.

Whatever one's condition, trust in God leads to a sense of blessedness. The Bible presents no romanticized picture of aging. The infirmities and anxieties of the old are realistically presented (Ps. 71:9,18; Eccl. 12:7). But God provides an antidote for the poisonous fear of old age: "For God hath not given us the spirit of fear; but of power, and love, and of a sound mind" (2 Tim. 1:7). There is also comfort in knowing "that all things [including the coming of old age] work together for good to them that love God, who are the called according to his purpose" (Rom. 8:28).

In a more general way the Bible tells us that all persons, regardless of age, productivity, beauty, or any other matter, are precious in God's sight. Old people, babies, and everyone in between are made in the image of God and are to be treated with respect. Christians are to love God, self, and others (Matt. 22:34–40). For an elderly Christian to despise himself because he is no longer "useful" is to violate Jesus' plain teaching. Furthermore, love is to be expressed not so much in word as in deed. Love is meeting the needs of other persons (Luke 10:25–37; 1 John 3:14–18). Since many of the aging have needs specifically mentioned and cared for by Jesus—hunger, loneliness, sickness, deafness, blindness, poverty—the Christian should be especially alert to meet those needs (Matt. 11:1–6; 25:31–46; Luke 4:16–21).

The Bible declares that the older Christian should neither fear death nor shirk living. Christ is preparing a place for every child of God and promises to care for all who trust him (John 14:1–4). One day all tears will be wiped away and there will be no more pain (Rev. 21:4). In the meantime, even suffering can be beneficial, though not necessarily pleasant (Col. 1:24; 1 Pet. 4:12–19). For the older persons without faith in Christ, life is desolate and the future is dark. The Bible pictures old age without obedience to God as symbolic of desolation (Ps. 90:10; Eccl. 11:8; 12:1–7; Jer. 6:11; Joel 1:2–3). This indicates that we should not be slack concerning evangelism and Christian nurture of older persons.

The older years should be looked upon as a part of life just as important and significant as any other period. Old age is part of God's plan for human life. Approached with a positive attitude, it can be as meaningful as any other time, perhaps more so. It is just as important to prepare for living well one's older years as for any other period in life.

Armed with the right outlook, we're ready for specific *action.* Without an adequate attitude about aging, most actions to prepare for older years or to minister to senior adults will be counterproductive.

As we prepare for church action for the aging, it is important to see them not so much as people in need of ministry— although many are—but as resources for Christian ministry to others. A key to effective church action is to work with, not just for, the older persons. Here is a rich, often untapped, resource for ministry.

Christian action related to aging falls into four basic categories—evangelism and Christian nurture, education, ministry to human need, and social change efforts. The truth is that many older people are lost, need Christ, and deserve a witness. Furthermore, the aging can benefit from Christian nurture. Growing old does not necessarily mean one automatically becomes more saintly. Bible study, prayer, meditation, Christian service—the fundamentals for Christian growth—are needed by the old as much as by any. They often respond enthusiastically to these.

Education concerning senior adults should be directed to *all* age groups. A fruitful old age is the result of a lifetime of preparation. People also need to be taught the proper attitude toward aging as well as the specific problems of old age and how to deal with them. Books, pamphlets, cassettes, filmstrips, and periodicals on aging should be available in every church's learning center. Most churches provide a children's section. Why not a senior adult section, including material in extra large print, items of special interest to retired persons, and cassettes for those with impaired eyesight?

A church can develop a galaxy of ministries to help meet the special needs of senior adults. A beginning place is the church building and routine program. Facilities should reflect concern for the aging—nonskid floors, well-lighted passageways, hearing aids in the pews, ramps for wheelchairs, elevators for those who can no longer climb stairs. Meetings for older persons can be scheduled at times and places convenient for them. Tapes of worship services, Bible study material, and other resources can be made available to the elderly who are confined to their home or an institution.

In addition, a church should identify the various needs of the aging and determine ways the church can help meet them. Teaching the biblical view of aging, utilizing senior adults in church programs, and relating to older persons in a manner that demonstrates interest, concern, and respect—these are some of the ways a church can meet the need for a sense of purpose and meaning in life. It is important for senior adults to do things for others and not for others to always be doing things for them. Games, busywork, and condescending visits won't do the job. The aging need to be taken seriously, though not necessarily solemnly.

A church can do many things to improve the health of senior citizens. Provide materials and conferences on proper health care. Maintain a well-elderly clinic. Inform persons about the benefits of Medicare and other programs that provide finances for health services. Operate a clinic with low or no cost medical and dental treatment. Establish a nursing home or help staff existing homes with volunteers. Develop a system of periodic visits to elderly persons by volunteer nurses or retired medical personnel.

Meals-on-wheels programs, cooking classes, providing materials on low-cost but nutritious meals, help with grocery buying—these are some ways churches can help with the nutrition problems of the elderly. A church might even encourage a group of older persons to form a co-op for buying foodstuffs in large quantities or establish a gardening group to grow produce for the elderly. For many, improper diet is due not to lack of money to buy food but lack of incentive to prepare and eat meals, especially when an older person lives alone. Group meals in church dining facilities help overcome this problem.

Since living in one's home is usually best for the senior adult, churches should help make this arrangement possible. Church-sponsored homemaker and handyman services can help cut the cost of maintaining a home. Counsel on improving the efficiency of heating and cooling and volunteer workers "tightening up" old houses can cut utility bills. Legal advice may save on taxes, loss from fraud, and unnecessary expenses. A telephone checkup service eases anxieties of an elderly person staying alone. When a senior adult is sick, the church can provide someone to help. For older persons living with grown children or others, a church can often assist by providing a sitter while the children must be gone.

Few cities have adequate public transport. Providing transportation for older persons can be a big help. A church-coordinated carpool is one means of assisting. Another is a church bus, especially equipped for the aging, to provide transportation. Church-related activities for the aging should include transportation service whenever needed.

No other institution is as well equipped as the church to

help persons face death. Church members can be taught the skills of ministering to the dying and the bereaved and then minister whenever the need arises. Lawyers can lead conferences on getting one's legal affairs in order prior to death—making a will, establishing trust funds, arranging for the disposition of one's body, and similar matters. The pastor can provide information on the Christian view of death, preparing for funeral arrangements, and Christian options for the use of one's body following death.

For those suffering from lingering terminal illnesses, Christians can give encouragement to look beyond the present pain to future joy. Without being either morbid or flippant, the child of God can deal realistically and hopefully with death.

One other factor is needed to deal effectively with the problems of the aging—efforts to bring about social change. Many senior citizens realize this and are working through organized effort to effect change. Christians of all ages should become informed and work to bring about social change to help the aging. Certainly numerous changes in business and political policy are called for by the plight of many of our nation's older citizens.

If Christians are going to do what we ought concerning the aging, we must believe the elderly are important. We tend to slight the old. We don't abuse them, but we sometimes subject them to benign neglect. When we fail to respond to the senior adults' needs we mirror our culture; we are worldy, not Godly.

If we believe the Bible as much as we say we do, we will not ignore older persons. If we follow Christ as ardently as we claim, we will minister to the needs of the elderly. If we are filled with the Spirit as we insist the Christian ought to be, we will reach out in love to the aging family. Let us be concrete and specific, not vaguely sentimental about this issue. Let our actions say to the world, and particularly to the aging family, that in Christ's name we care.

12

Handling the Holidays
(Christmas)

And when he was twelve years old, they went up to Jerusalem after the custom of the feast.

And when they had fulfilled the days, as they returned, the child Jesus tarried behind in Jerusalem; and Joseph and his mother knew not of it.

But they, supposing him to have been in the company, went a day's journey; and they sought him among their kinsfolk and acquaintance.

And when they found him not, they turned back again to Jerusalem, seeking him.

And it came to pass, that after three days they found him in the temple, sitting in the midst of the doctors, both hearing them, and asking them questions.

And all that heard him were astonished at his understanding and answers.

And when they saw him, they were amazed: and his mother said unto him, Son, why hast thou thus dealt with us? behold, thy father and I have sought thee sorrowing.

And he said unto them, How is it that ye sought me? wist ye not that I must be about my Father's business?

And they understood not the saying which he spake unto them.

And he went down with them, and came to Nazareth, and was subject unto them: but his mother kept all these sayings in her heart.

And Jesus increased in wisdom and stature, and in favour with God and man (Luke 2:42–52).

Do you know people who have all their Christmas cards addressed by the Fourth of July, with zip code affixed, ready to mail? By Labor Day all their Christmas shopping is done.

120

By Halloween all their presents are wrapped, and those to distant relatives are in the mail. On Thanksgiving they take out neatly stored Christmas decorations and place them carefully throughout the house—and there's not a tangled string of lights to be found. Precisely two weeks before Christmas they purchase and decorate the tree and put the packages underneath. A week before Christmas the menu for the big meal is planned, all food purchased, and most of the baking done. The week before Christmas is relaxed and calm.

Frankly, I've never known any families like that. There may be some; but those I know discover that as the holiday season moves into full gear, their lives become more and more hectic. Some even long for Christmas to be over so that they can return to a degree of normalcy. People who are usually rather cheerful become sullen. The season to be jolly becomes a frantic series of crises. What is supposed to be the best of times for families can turn into the worst of times. There are many reasons why.

For one thing, at this season we are faced with deadline after deadline and constantly reminded of each one. The media massages us with the messages. The post office says, "Get your cards and letters in; only packages mailed before a certain date will arrive on time." The stores say, "Only ten shopping days left until Christmas; buy now." The choir director says, "Sunday night is the performance. You've got to be here; you've got to be ready." The family asks, "When will we eat? What will we eat? Where are we spending the holidays?" Friends ask, "You will come to our party, won't you?" Soon the barrage of deadlines and meetings and rehearsals and parties and programs takes its toll. We feel like a shell-shocked victim of the front lines.

Another thing happens. Our routines—and routine is a rather comfortable way to live—are broken. Schoolteachers are particularly aware of this. The routine of the classroom is disrupted with the coming of the Christmas season. Students who are normally controllable become wild. Teachers who can usually discipline their emotions begin to look for a padded cell.

The family's routine is mangled by a series of special events. Most well-ordered families, for example, have a routine about television—which programs and how many hours of television to watch. Suddenly, with numerous television specials, family arguments erupt about what will be watched. The routine is broken. Most families usually care about health and follow a sensible diet. Holiday food, parties, and banquets change eating patterns. The high intake of sweets takes its toll. With bodies already tending toward obesity, we consume food that adds pounds and fills our cardiovascular system with death-dealing substances. We feel stuffed and lethargic; sometimes our bodies develop a kind of dull ache.

Another cause of holiday havoc is the expense. Panic seizes some when they realize that expenses are mounting more rapidly than they anticipated. They go into a dime store to buy something and discover that nothing costs a dime anymore. They go into a toy shop to buy a few items and are attracted to more than they planned to buy. Mom and Dad begin to panic as the bills pile up; but they don't want to look cheap, so they spend more than they intended and feel trapped and frustrated.

Sometimes travel is the cause of holiday jitters. People go from their own comfortable surroundings to unfamiliar places. Houses filled to capacity put a strain on plumbing, bathroom, and kitchen facilities. Strange beds and new sounds make sleeping difficult. Family feuds smoldering for months may burst into open confrontations. Children play—and sometimes fight—noisily. Soon grandparents, who really *do* love their grandchildren, begin to look forward to the time when there will be peace and quiet on the home front again.

For many families there is the added burden of an empty chair during the holidays. Since last Christmas someone very dear has died—a daddy, mother, husband, wife, son, or daughter. Or divorce has broken the family apart. At this particular time of the year the absence of the voice, smile, and laughter of the person gone is particularly noticed. Under the Christmas tree where presents for the loved one rested last year, there are none. Such a void is difficult to cope with—especially when people all around are sending messages of good cheer and you don't feel cheerful at all. Having the environment surrounding you totally different from the way you feel is a miserable experience. It's no wonder that during the holidays the number of suicides soar, depression is rampant, and anxiety symptoms are everywhere.

You may feel I'm sounding like Scrooge in *A Christmas Carol* with a "Bah humbug!" whenever Christmas is mentioned. That's not my attitude at all. I love Christmas. But I believe those of us who wear the label "Christian" must learn to handle the holidays better, or we will do more damage to the cause of Christ than good.

How should a Christian family handle the holidays? It will help if we are aware of the pitfalls and make preparations to avoid them. By doing advance planning together and making some agreements, a family can eliminate many of the problems. They can agree, for example, to maintain a strong devotional life, keep activity to a manageable level, eat sensibly, and rest adequately. It is also important to remember that the word *holiday* comes from *holy day* and that this holiday won't be a holy day if it is characterized by frantic activity, enormous expense, and gluttonous behavior.

Let this be a "holy day" season, a special period dedicated to God. Let Christmas be a day set aside for rest from one's normal routine, for worship and celebration of God's presence, for disengagement from the routine. Let our energies center on him, the Lord God Almighty. That's the answer, really, to handling the holidays. It's to get in perspective what this season is all about, to major on the One whose name is in the midst of it, the Christ of Christmas. As we concentrate on him and his way, much of that which drags us down to the pit of despair or rips us apart in frantic activity will affect us no more. Then we can put life together in wholeness.

But this answer to handling the holidays can actually be part of the problem. In an effort to concentrate on Christ we may major on church activity, expecting that to bring peace to the stormy waters of the season. If we are not careful that will only add to the problem. In church it is possible to lose the Christ who alone can bring us peace. Could that be why Luke coupled the story about Jesus lost from his parents in the Temple with the story of the nativity?

The Christ found by the shepherds in the manger and later adored by the Wise Men was lost by his own parents in the Temple. We can lose him there, too. Quite often people come to the temple—to the church house—in the midst of the holiday season, but their minds are not on him. Their thoughts are on something else. Distracted, they lose the Christ whom they have come to celebrate.

Mary and Joseph lost Jesus in the house of God during a holiday, a "holy day" season. It was the Passover, and people had gathered from all over the country to celebrate, much as we gather during Christmas. They celebrated the event when God allowed the angel of death to pass over Israel and then led them through the sea to freedom. It was a time for families to get together, travel, and visit. It was a time to renew old acquaintances and to make new friends, much like our season. It was also a time for worship. Many people came to the Temple, the holiest place in all of Israel, for the Passover. They came to Jerusalem, the Holy City. But in the Temple, in the midst of the Holy City, during the sacred Passover season, Mary and Joseph lost Jesus, the Son of God. Some of us have lost Jesus too. And in losing him—not in the sense of losing our salvation, but of losing a close, wonderful relation with him—we lose all the real worth of this season.

Mary and Joseph didn't lose Jesus because they disliked him. They didn't lose Jesus because they were weary of him. They didn't lose Jesus because they were angry with him, any more than most of us do. They lost him the same way we usually do—through indifference and neglect. They lost him because their attention was fixed on something else. Distracted by the activity of the city and the preparation to return home, with a thousand plans to make, they simply forgot about him.

Of course, they didn't totally forget about him. Mary probably thought he was with Joseph and Joseph thought he was with Mary. But the fact they didn't check on him indicates neglect or distraction. They depended on somebody else to see to it that Jesus was present, just like many people depend upon the professional religionist to see that Jesus is present in this season of the year. But each of us is responsible for a close personal relation to Jesus.

Mary and Joseph lost him the way many of us lose him—distraction, busyness, neglect. Preoccupied with cards to get out, dinners to fix, presents to buy, people to contact, places to go, plans to make—we forget him. We can travel a long way before we realize he's gone. Mary and Joseph did. We can be involved in worship services, music programs, and dramatic events depicting the first Christmas. We can sing Christmas carols, view manger scenes, and participate in a galaxy of Christmas events, feeling that he is surely with us, when suddenly in a rare moment of contemplation we realize he's gone. He's not with us. We've walked away and left him.

How do you find him? By going to where he is, among people who care about him and listen to him and respond to his love—among people who are in fellowship with him. You will find him where people gather to truly worship God. In a world frantic with the activity of the season, but forgetful about the Christ, the most likely place to find him is among Christians who love him and want to spend time with him.

You may find him in a godly family where people have not allowed themselves to be distracted by all the tinsel of the season, but have kept their attention focused upon the Christ. You may find him in the life of a godly person who, although he may enjoy the carols and the lights and the festivity, doesn't allow these to crowd Jesus out of his life. You'll find him in fellowship and worship. You'll find him where people are gathered around the Word of God to study.

When you find him you'll discover that your life, shattered into a hundred disjointed fragments, comes together again around him. When life has lost its zest, when the holidays have lost their holiness, when the season of good cheer has become a time of frustration, when joy has escaped, when your body aches and your head throbs, Christmas can become good news if you will find Jesus and center your life in him. Around the Christ you gain perspective. Wholeness is reestablished. You begin to understand the true meaning of Christmas, God's giving the gift of his Son. The way to begin to right what is wrong about this season is for your family to put him first.

Is your family life a shambles, your home a madhouse? Are you so busy that life has become one deadline, one bleary-eyed meeting, one social event, one practice, one get-together, one worship service after another? Then put Jesus back in the center of your life. Have you noticed that at this time of the year we tend to neglect our quiet times with the Father? We are so busy being religious that we don't have time to be Christian at Christmas. So frantic are we that the disciplines of Bible study, quiet time, and prayer are dissipated when we need them most. Begin each day with him—pondering, meditating, praying, communing, fellowshipping—finding him where people find him: around the Word of God.

Is materialism ruining the season for you? Do you feel smothered in an effort to get and give impressively? Then find Jesus and learn from him. Jesus gave himself for us. He calls us to give ourselves and all that we have to God. The Wise Men brought their gifts to the Christ child. At this season we are to bring our gifts to him too—our lives, talents, resources, time, and money.

It's good to give gifts to other people if it's for the right reason; if you want to share out of love something that is really part of you. But remember, the cure for the materialism that afflicts many at Christmas is to pour our resources into the channel of God's work in the world; to spend far more on the cause of evangelism and missions than we do on anything else at this time of year; to see that what we give to family and friends is multiplied manifold in our gifts to a lost and needy world. If you will do that, you and your family will find real joy in your giving this Christmas.

Is the season being spoiled by the loneliness that comes when loved ones are gone? Is there an empty chair at your table this year? Are you beginning to feel teary and depressed to the point that you don't even want to think about Christmas? Then find Jesus. Go where he is. Put your life around his Word and begin to listen once more to the promises he makes. "Fear not, I am with you always." "Let not your heart be troubled: ye believe in God, believe also in me." As you draw close to him, he pushes out the loneliness, eases the grief, and wipes away the tears.

When Mary and Joseph found Jesus, he told them, "I must be about my Father's business." The implication was clear: Mary and Joseph were to be about the Father's business too. So are we. And when we are, we will find Jesus, we will be with him. That's the best way to find and be with him, to be about the Father's business. When you are worshiping, ministering, evangelizing—you are about his business. The one who said, "I must be about my Father's business" also said, "Follow me" (Matt. 14:19). When we do, we discover that he has made us part of the greatest adventure of all time. God, who could have won the world without us, has chosen to do it with us. Jesus calls us to be co-workers in his mission to a lost world. Remember his words "As my Father hath sent me, even so send I you" (John 20:21).

If you really want to make Christmas joyful as a family, then be about his business. Spend your time sharing the good news about Jesus Christ. Tell people that the story doesn't end in a Bethlehem manger; it continues on the cross of Calvary and at a tomb torn open by the power of God. Tell them it didn't end with the angels' message to a group of shepherds; it continues with the account of Jesus' ascension and his words "Ye shall be witnesses unto me" (Acts 1:8). The best way to handle the holidays is to make them holy days, days set aside to major on the Father's business. The best gift we share is the gift of the gospel; the best carol ever sung is the song of the redeemed. When you begin to celebrate Christmas in that way, it becomes a wonderful adventure. What is the answer to the frustration so many feel in this season of the year? Finding Jesus and hearing him say, "I must be about my Father's business. Follow me!"

Christmas doesn't have to be a catastrophe. It can be the best time of the year, but it won't be if you and I allow our family to be pushed along by the practices of our society. It can be a wonderful season if we will find and follow the Jesus whom many have lost along the way.

You're not a Christian? Then the best Christmas of all will be when you give yourself to the Christ who gave himself for you. No better present could you give your family and yourself than to give your life to Jesus in faith and trust. What joy there will be in your home this Christmas if every member of the family is a member of the family of God. The time before Christmas will likely be the best or the worst of the year for you. The outcome depends on whether you find Jesus and make your top priority staying close to him, joining him in being about the Father's business. If you do, it will be a Merry Christmas indeed.

How to Conduct
Family Ministry
in a Local Church

Family life is God's creation, his gift to mankind. The gifts God grants to his people are good; he intended family to be for our joy, not our hurt. Like any other good gift, family life can be abused or misused. When that happens, it works for the harm and not the help of family members. If family is to bring the happiness it was designed to provide, family members need to know and follow God's guidelines for family living.

The Bible is God's word to us about life and how to live it, including family life. In the Bible are found the basic truths about what families are for and the guidelines concerning how they are to function. Sharing these biblical teachings is important for strengthening family life. The responsibility for such sharing rests with church and family leaders. Every pastor, church staff person, Sunday School teacher, and Christian family member has an opportunity to discover and share the biblical truth about family life. Outside experts on family life can be brought in from time to time, but the main responsibility rests with the church family's own members, especially with the pastor.

Background

Effective communication of what the Bible teaches about family will come out of a background not only of careful biblical study but also extensive involvement in family life and ministry. The person who is either in an office studying or on a platform speaking most of the time, who does not participate in his own family's life or relate to the families of others, isn't likely to be an effective communicator about family life.

Participating in one's own family provides a background of personal experience. When a person sees biblical truth at work for good in his own marriage, he wants to share the truth with others. Theology comes alive in family recreation and worship. By being active in one's own family, a person sets an example for those who listen to his teaching about family. Credibility is low when a man talks about the importance of family life but by his actions demonstrates he really doesn't consider his own family to be very important. What is called for is not perfect family life—no one achieves that— but a model of family involvement, an example of a person who places family high on his list of priorities.

Helping develop an extensive family ministry also increases the credibility of the one who shares biblical truth about family. A pastor who preaches eloquent, biblical sermons about family life but does little more than that to help families will leave many people wondering if he really believes what he preaches. The spokesman about family crises who is also the minister to families in crisis will be more readily heard. Furthermore, he will speak in a way more directly related to life if he in fact does relate directly to the families in the church and community. Counseling families in distress, visiting the ill and grief-stricken, going with the youth on retreats and listening to them talk, spending time in nursing homes— these are the kinds of experiences that help keep talk about family rooted in reality.

A total ministry to families is also a way of saying, "I really care about family life." Talk is cheap. Anyone can rattle off Scriptures and stories about what families ought to be. But organizing programs and structures to help families takes time, hard work, planning, and plenty of effort. It's worth it, though. Not only are families better helped, but words about family are more readily heard and responded to.

A church's ministry to families will take on different forms according to needs, location, and resources. But certain things are needed practically everywhere. One is a basic understanding of what family life is really like in the community and what needs are present. A church ought to find out the answers to questions such as these:

1. What resources are available in the community to help families?

2. What recreational programs and facilities are available to youth? Are these adequate?

3. Are there organizations that can provide special help for one-parent families?

4. Are family counseling services available in the community?

5. Is adequate prenatal and postnatal medical care and diet available to all who need it?

6. What provisions are available for the aging in food, housing, transportation, medical care, recreation, and financial support?

7. Is there adequate housing for low-income individuals and families?

8. Are all children in the community receiving adequate nutrition, health care, and education?

9. Does the welfare system in your state support or undermine family life? How?

10. What provisions are available for children of mothers who work outside the home?

11. What is the rate of divorce in your community? delinquency? crime?

Based on needs, church programs can be developed to enrich family life. Some programs could major on education or information about family life, such as the following:

1. Provide group-sharing sessions, conferences, and retreats for those with common interests, such as youth facing marriage, the divorced, the widowed, newlyweds, parents of teenagers, couples whose children are grown, couples facing retirement, and the aged.

2. Supply families with materials geared to meet specific

needs. For example, when a family has a child who reaches his thirteenth birthday, send them material on parent-teen relations.

3. Sponsor family life conferences for the entire community, holding some of the meetings in locations other than the church.

4. Arrange for Bible study and discussion groups on family life for various ages.

5. Observe Christian Home Week each year.

6. Offer sex education programs and premarital counseling.

7. Keep a tract rack filled with helpful, attractive material on family life.

8. Purchase good books for the church library on different phases of family life.

9. Stock waiting rooms at bus stations, hospitals, and doctors' offices with attractive, current, helpful material on family life.

10. Sponsor a radio program, television program, or newspaper column on advice for successful family living.

11. Take groups of church members through slum areas and lead them in a discussion of what can be done to improve the situation so as to benefit family life.

Other programs might be more action-oriented, such as these:

1. Coordinate church meetings to avoid taking families out of the home more often than necessary for church activities.

2. Provide counseling service for families in stress.

3. Develop a child-care center for the children of mothers who work outside the home.

4. Provide after-school recreation and tutoring for children of working mothers.

5. Encourage public and private organizations to make available adequate recreational facilities, especially for adults and children from poverty areas.

6. Purchase camping and/or recreational facilities and schedule families to use these facilities.

7. Offer courses in cooking, sewing, and child care, especially for poor families.

8. Initiate programs to improve housing for low-income families.

9. Form nonprofit private corporations to build or rehabilitate low-cost housing.

10. Work for the kind of welfare programs that help to maintain stable family life.

11. Support strict enforcement of the housing and sanitation codes.

12. Work to develop public and private programs that ensure the needy aging of adequate food, clothing, shelter, and health care.

Teaching and preaching about family life will be much more effective when done against a background of family ministry than when done apart from a practical demonstration of concern about family enrichment.

In the First Baptist Church of Wichita Falls those of us in leadership tried to demonstrate concern for family life. For example, a full-time staff member, the minister of family enrichment, was employed to direct various programs of family enrichment, coordinate the deacons' family ministry, provide a counseling service, and aid families in crisis. The recreation director developed a recreation program for families, singles, and senior adults. The Children's director and Preschool director conducted workshops on parent-child relations. The minister of youth developed programs to improve parent-teenage relations. Sunday School departments held marriage enrichment retreats. Church Training included sessions on family life. A cassette ministry included excellent family enrichment material. The church library and book store stocked a wide variety of books on family life. Hundreds of people played an active role in family ministry.

The program of family enrichment in our church taught

me many things. One of the most important was that family enrichment calls for more than sermons and lectures on family life. It calls for guided action, small-group discussions, role play, and various other methods to help people learn how to relate to one another in positive ways. You don't learn to relate to others through the lecture method; you learn by doing, under guidance of a skilled supervisor. That insight didn't cause me to stop preaching and teaching; sermons and lectures can be helpful. It did help me realize their limitations.

Issues and Topics

In sharing biblical truth about family life a checklist of various topics is helpful. When we use a checklist important subjects won't be overlooked. Each person should work out his own list, but this one I've found helpful:

1. According to the Family Cycle
    a. Premarriage—dating, personality development, sexuality, goals, values.
    b. Marriage—choosing a mate, premarital counseling, engagement, wedding, honeymoon.
    c. Early Marriage—adjustments, relation to in-laws, communication, finances, roles, family worship.
    d. Parenting—childhood development, parent-child relations, discipline, supervision, self-image, authority, moral values.
    e. The Empty Nest—parent-teenage tension, children leaving home, marriage of children, middle-age adjustments.
    f. Preretirement—role changes, finances, health, plans for retirement, care for aging parents.
    g. Retirement—finances, emotional strain, time usage, relation to children and grandchildren, place to live, security, health, death of spouse, living alone, preparing for death.
    h. Becoming single—dealing with grief, adjustment to

aloneness, handling negative emotions such as guilt, anger, or low self-esteem.
2. According to the Type of Family Unit
   a. Single Adults—companionship, self-image in a marriage-oriented society, sexuality, marriage.
   b. Single Parent—finances, parent-child relation, relation to ex-spouse for those who are divorced, learning to parent alone, dating and remarriage, grief and/or anger toward ex-spouse.
   c. Blended Family (children from more than one marriage)—relation of children to absent parent, agreement between parents on childrearing principles, comparisons with ex-spouse parent, relation to in-laws from different families.
   d. Childless Couple—decision about having children, decision about options (adoption, foster care), relationship to families with children dealing with guilt and/or anger about childlessness.
   e. Nuclear Family (father, mother, children)—husband-wife communication, parent-child communication, money management, time management, agreement on role, relation with in-laws, sexual adjustment, spiritual development.
   f. Minority Family (ethnic or language)—decision about cultural identification, dealing with prejudice and discrimination, language problems, feelings of worth.
   g. Poverty-stricken Family—inadequate food, clothing, and housing, self-image, lack of privacy, safety, working parents.
   h. Wealthy Family—developing work habits in children, time for family togetherness, stewardship of possessions and power.
   i. Mobile Family (migrants, military, businessmen who are transferred often, etc.)—sense of rootlessness, ad-

justing to new areas, developing in-depth friendships, security.

j. Aging Family—health, finances, sense of being needed, fear of dependence, relation to children, grief.

3. According to Family Relationships
   a. Husband-Wife—communication, roles, sexual adjustment, values, time together, conflict resolution.
   b. Parent-Child—nurture, supervision, discipline, communication, time together, spiritual development.
   c. Child-Child—sibling rivalry, self-image, sense of worth, lack of feeling of being loved.
   d. Family-In-Laws—childrearing, holidays, finances, values.
4. According to Topics or Issues
   a. Communication between husband and wife.
   b. Communication between parents and children.
   c. Christian commitment, growth, and family worship.
   d. Values, goals, and ideals.
   e. Conflict management.
   f. Finances, budgets.
   g. Understanding and dealing with teenagers.
   h. Time together as a family.
   i. Sexuality.
   j. Church involvement.
   k. Roles and authority.
   l. Discipline and supervision of children.
   m. Both parents working outside the home.
   n. Family planning and decisions.
   o. Relation to in-laws.
   p. Recreation, movies, television.
   q. Birth control and planned parenthood.
   r. Grief related to death, moves, failures.
   s. Health, diet, exercise.
   t. Care for aging parents.
   u. Interfaith marriages.

     v. Marriage of children.
     w. Divorce and remarriage.
5. According to Basic Family Needs
     a. Understanding the nature and purpose of marriage and family.
     b. Setting goals for family life.
     c. Developing skills in family members for good family life.
     d. Dealing with failures in the family.

These are not exhaustive lists of family-related topics, but they do demonstrate the wide variety of subjects that need to be covered.

Another approach to developing a checklist for sharing biblical truth about family would be to list all the passages from the Bible on family, group them according to topics, and use this collection of Scriptures as a basis for sharing. A partial group of such Scriptures is found in this book. By combining topics with texts, you will have a list of all the basic subjects about marriage and family with which you need to deal.

Method

What methods should be used to share biblical truth about family life? The form of communication can take a variety of shapes. Sermons and talks are only two of many forms. Sermons followed by dialogue with the listeners is a useful variation. Some have found it helpful to meet with a small group of persons to discuss the approach and content of a sermon *before* it is preached. Informal talks using audiovisual materials, movies, filmstrips, cassettes, and role play are often effective.

Truth about family can be shared in written as well as spoken form. Sermons on family can be transcribed, printed, and distributed. Articles in the church paper can stress family life. Tracts on family can be distributed in worship services, in meetings, or through the mail. The church library or book store can stock materials on family life. Letters written to persons at key points in their family's life can be effective—at the birth of a child, on a wedding anniversary, at a death and on the anniversary of a death, at the marriage of a son or daughter, at the time of a move, during a major illness.

Any method of communicating about family life should take advantage of every opportunity to make an input to families. Sunday worship times, Wednesday night services, Bible studies, Church Training groups, conferences, seminars, retreats—all sorts of settings are suitable. Many events and occasions are ready-made for a family emphasis—Christian Home Week, Mother's Day, Father's Day, Parent Dedication Day, Senior Adult Day, commencements, weddings, funerals, Bible studies, and holidays.

Other events during the year provide an opportunity for a family emphasis—revivals, stewardship campaigns, doctrinal studies, discipleship emphases, Vacation Bible School, youth retreats, Church Training sessions, women's and men's meetings. Family-related illustrations can be used in conjunction with sermons, emphases, and studies on almost any subject. For example, a sermon on the doctrine of God could contain a family-type illustration related to God as heavenly Father.

Guiding Principles

In examining numerous and varied communications on family life, I have discovered certain common characteristics. Not that all sharing on family is alike. It isn't. For example, in sermons some take a verse-by-verse approach, while others use a topical system. Some go heavy on sociological and psychological insights, while others stress biblical exegesis. Some are problem-centered and others are goal-centered. Some follow strict outline procedure, while others use narrative, dialogue, or a flow of ideas. Some often utilize audiovisuals, while others almost never do. Some are dynamic in their style; others are quiet and subdued.

With all these differences there are nonetheless some common factors in effective communication about family life. First, the material is thoroughly biblical. Some quote a great deal of Scripture, and others summarize biblical truth; but all base what they say about the family on the Bible. Insights from the social sciences may be used; but the Bible, not the social sciences, is their source of authority. They may differ in their interpretation of what the Bible teaches about certain aspects of family life, but they go to the Bible for their standards and not to public-opinion polls or the views of secular spokesmen. The biblical teachings are applied to daily life in a thoroughly practical, down-to-earth kind of way.

Second, the material contains a positive emphasis. Effective communicators don't merely present the problems; they offer solutions. They don't criticize families for failure; they offer positive suggestions for correcting weaknesses. Their emphasis is not so much on how families get sick as on how healthy families can get better. Prevention rather than correction is their theme. Family enrichment is their dominant note.

Outstanding communicators keep a balance between describing how to deal with family problems and how to set family goals. Problems can't be ignored; all families have problems. Often, however, the best way to deal with a problem is to prevent it from developing; that calls for positive action. A continuing emphasis is needed on what constitutes healthy families, on what ingredients must be present for families to be whole and happy. A steady diet of problem-centered family communication can be depressing. What's right with families ought to be stressed. Illustrations of sound family life ought to be sprinkled through everything that is said.

Third, the communication contains a balance of evangelistic and pastoral emphases. No one can have a Christian home unless he or she is a Christian. Evangelism is necessary for stable family life. The family that is part of the family of God has more opportunity for genuine happiness than the one that isn't. Yet becoming a Christian doesn't eliminate all of a person's problems. Similarly, having a Christian home doesn't eliminate all of a family's problems. Pastoral care in word and deed is essential to a family's health. Communication based on the Bible should deal both with how members of a family can be saved and with how saved members of a family are to live. Resources on coping with family needs should constantly be set forth from the Word of God.

Pitfalls

At one time I thought communicating about family life was the least perilous, easiest kind of Christian communication. Since then I've learned better. It may not be as explosive as dealing with race relations, economic issues, or political matters; but it is certainly not immune to controversy. When you proclaim biblical truth on family, be prepared for heated, emotional reaction. Handle what you say and the response you evoke with care; you are dealing with an explosive subject.

Why is family life such a controversial and emotional subject? Most persons have strong opinions about family topics—how to raise children, remarriage after divorce, and sexuality, for example—and if your views don't coincide with theirs, they'll react strongly. Many people have tender scars from past family crises; they are sensitive to emphases on what family life ought to be. Those in the midst of serious family difficulty may feel that any family-centered communication is directed toward them or that such a message draws attention to their plight, and they don't like it.

Recent developments have made the field of family life much more controversial than it has been in the past. Popular seminars attended by thousands have stressed an approach to family structure and authority that many other family experts find unbiblical and harmful. Widely read material on women has majored on the submissive role of women, while other extensive material has emphasized the need for women's rights and liberation. Battle lines have been drawn over the nature and function of family. Anyone who deals with family will find himself in the crossfire between opposing camps.

All of this does not mean that the Christian communicator should avoid dealing with family life. To the contrary, it makes speaking to family issues even more important. It does mean that a person should be aware of the pitfalls and strive to make a positive contribution, not simply to stir controversy. How can this be done?

First, do your homework. Make certain that statistics are accurate and up to date. If you use quotations, be sure you quote correctly and are aware of the context of the quote. Carefully exegete and interpret all Scripture passages used. Many people have studied widely in the family field and will be aware of mistakes you make. It won't take many errors on your part to seriously damage your credibility. Read carefully what outstanding Christian writers say about family life.

Second, remember that you are dealing with sensitive subjects. Many people listening to you have been badly scarred by family difficulties. Some are going through nasty divorce proceedings. Some have recently lost a spouse to death. Some are experiencing grief from a wayward son or daughter. Some live daily with the pain of a badly functioning marriage. Deal tenderly with persons as you share biblical truth about family.

Third, in addition to holding up standards for family life, also describe how to reach the standards and how to deal with failure to reach them. Many people dismiss emphases on family as too idealistic or unrealistic because they present simplistic solutions to very complex problems. Pew sitters sometimes get the impression that the pulpit pounder just doesn't understand the way things really are, that he lives in a world apart, that he doesn't comprehend the problems of mere mortals. Confessional preaching can help correct such a misunderstanding. By confessing his own problems, sense of frustration, and failures, the Christian communicator can establish a relation with his listeners. He can still hold high the standards of the biblical revelation and show how God in Christ meets human need; but he does it out of the context of being human, of understanding people's problems.

Setting forth the standard without describing in practical terms how to reach it leads to frustration. Telling people they have fallen short of God's goal for family life comes as no surprise; we all realize we have sinned and fallen short of God's standard. What many don't know is how to make progress toward the goal, how to do a better job. What we need to know is what to do when we fail. How should we handle the guilt?

Fourth, avoid using illustrations from family counseling sessions or from your own family life. It's perfectly permissible to utilize insights gained in counseling and family involvement, but not specific accounts or stories. Illustrations from the lives of counselees may scare persons away who need help; they fear that they too will become a sermon illustration.

Illustrations from one's own family can embarrass family members, cause them problems in relating to others, and undermine family stability. If an illustration from your own family is used, be sure it is a positive one. Putting down members of your family in public, making fun of them, using them as the butt of jokes, and ridiculing their actions is not only bad taste; it is destructive of good family relations. Even if an illustration is positive in nature, it's a good idea to clear the idea with the people involved before using it.

Conclusion

Few exercises in Christian communication are more challenging and demanding—and rewarding and satisfying—than those dealing with marriage and family. No better opportunity exists to share the gospel than in the context of a message on family because you speak to where people live every day. Not everyone will be vitally interested in a word about infant baptism, but just about everybody will be interested in an emphasis on how to have a better family. Demonstrating that the Bible speaks to family life will heighten an interest in Bible study. Showing how the gospel can help a person cope with the demands of family life will increase a person's interest in the gospel. No more effective evangelistic and pastoral proclamation can occur than that related to family life.

In preparing the thirteen-volume *Twenty Centuries of Great Preaching*, Clyde Fant and I discovered that the effective communicators of biblical truth dealt frequently with marriage and family life and that the great churches majored on strengthening families. As I taught biblical ethics in a seminary for twelve years, I was continually impressed by the amount of material in the Bible on family life. Since God felt it important to include these passages in his inspired Word, we ought to consider them important in the proclamation of that Word. As a pastor I daily discovered no greater felt need on the part of people than in the area of family life; Christ commanded us to minister to need. And we should not, must not, ignore family life. As an administrator in contact with persons from many walks of life and parts of the world, I note how family life affects all that we do. As a researcher in church growth, I observe that healthy, growing churches are those that strive to meet the needs of families.

From study, background, and experience, I am convinced that marriage and family life must play a key part in our communication and application of biblical truth. The sermons in this volume are offered out of that conviction. They are not models of perfection in preaching. They don't cover all aspects of family life. They fall short of perfectly illustrating what I've set forth in this chapter.

This book represents an effort by a pastor to share God's truth with persons to help them improve their family life. I'm grateful for the increasing amount of material being published on family life that provides helpful insight from a biblical perspective on practically all aspects of family life. They, along with books such as this, ought to help us all do a better job of sharing biblical truth on marriage and family life.

Remember, such sharing is every Christian's responsibility. The principles set forth in this chapter apply to a father or mother sharing with their children, a husband and wife sharing with each other, a Sunday School teacher sharing with a class. Every church member can play a role in developing a strong church family enrichment program. If our families are to become what God intended—families with purpose—all of us must help each other by sharing insights from the Bible and encouraging one another to apply them to life.

Scripture and Family

The Bible contains hundreds of passages related to family life. Some of the Scriptures are historical descriptions of family life, good and bad. The Bible is realistic and shows family life at its worst—incest, adultery, dishonesty—and at its best—love, faithfulness, worship. We are not to follow all of the examples of family recorded in the Bible. We should not practice polygamy or own slaves or cheat our relatives. But we can learn from the accounts of family life, good and bad.

Other Scriptures are laws that God gave Israel to guide family relationships. Some are harsh: a rebellious youth was to be stoned to death; an adulterer was to be executed. Many relate to practices common then, but not now, such as laws regulating the marriage of priests, the treatment of married slaves, and the responsibility of a man to have children by his deceased brother's widow. Truth can be learned from these laws even though we no longer follow them. We don't follow the Old Testament rules for animal sacrifice, but we learn something from them about sin and atonement. It is against our laws to kill a rebellious son, but this Old Testament law teaches us about the seriousness of parent-child relations.

Many passages apply directly to us today, however. Guidelines and principles abound in the Bible on the relation of husband and wife, parent and child. Scriptures on certain subjects, such as divorce, must be carefully interpreted. Faithful Christians differ on the meaning of certain passages. Yet

145

in spite of the differences, it is important for Christians to take their standards for marriage and family from the Bible and not from society. Those preaching and teaching on family must be careful to distinguish what the Bible says about family from what the Bible teaches about family and must set forth the basic biblical standards in contrast to the custom of society.

The following passages are selected from hundreds related to marriage and family. Some are historical descriptions; others are the laws for Israel; most are timeless teachings; all provide insight about God's standards for family life. I have grouped them according to key aspects of family; a dozen other topics could have been used. The Bible is a rich mine for discovering treasures of guidance for persons who want better families—families with purpose.

Marriage

And the Lord God said, It is not good that the man should be alone; I will make him an help meet for him.

And out of the ground the Lord God formed every beast of the field, and every fowl of the air; and brought them unto Adam to see what he would call them: and whatsoever Adam called every living creature, that was the name thereof.

And Adam gave names to all cattle, and to the fowl of the air, and to every beast of the field; but for Adam there was not found an help meet for him.

And the Lord God caused a deep sleep to fall upon Adam, and he slept: and he took one of his ribs, and closed up the flesh instead thereof;

And the rib, which the Lord God had taken from man, made he a woman, and brought her unto the man.

And Adam said, This is now bone of my bones, and flesh of my flesh: she shall be called Woman, because she was taken out of Man.

Therefore shall a man leave his father and his mother, and shall cleave unto his wife: and they shall be one flesh (Gen. 2:18–24).

Whoso findeth a wife findeth a good thing, and obtaineth favour of the Lord (Prov. 18:22).

Take ye wives, and beget sons and daughters; and take wives for your sons, and give your daughters to husbands, that they may bear sons and daughters; that ye may be increased there, and not diminished (Jer. 29:6).

The same day came to him the Sadducees, which say that there is no resurrection, and asked him,

Saying, Master, Moses said, If a man die, having no children, his brother shall marry his wife, and raise up seed unto his brother.

Now there were with us seven brethren: and the first, when he had married a wife, deceased, and, having no issue, left his wife unto his brother:

Likewise the second also, and the third, unto the seventh.

And last of all the woman died also.

Therefore in the resurrection whose wife shall she be of the seven? for they all had her.

Jesus answered and said unto them, Ye do err, not knowing the scriptures, nor the power of God.

For in the resurrection they neither marry, nor are given in marriage, but are as the angels of God in heaven (Matt. 22:23–30).

Know ye not, brethren, (for I speak to them that know the law,) how that the law hath dominion over a man as long as he liveth?

For the woman which hath an husband is bound by the law to her husband so long as he liveth; but if the husband be dead, she is loosed from the law of her husband.

So then if, while her husband liveth, she be married to another man, she shall be called an adulteress: but if her husband be dead, she is free from that law; so that she is no adulteress, though she be married to another man (Rom. 7:1–3).

I say therefore to the unmarried and widows, It is good for them if they abide even as I.

But if they cannot contain, let them marry: for it is better to marry than to burn (1 Cor. 7:8–9).

Now concerning virgins I have no commandment of the Lord: yet I give my judgment, as one that hath obtained mercy of the Lord to be faithful.

I suppose therefore that this is good for the present distress, I say, that it is good for a man so to be.

Art thou bound unto a wife? seek not to be loosed. Art thou loosed from a wife? seek not a wife.

But and if thou marry, thou hast not sinned; and if a virgin marry, she hath not sinned. Nevertheless such shall have trouble in the flesh: but I spare you.

But this I say, brethren, the time is short: it remaineth, that both they that have wives be as though they had none;

And they that weep, as though they wept not; and they that rejoice, as though they rejoiced not; and they that buy, as though they possessed not;

And they that use this world, as not abusing it: for the fashion of this world passeth away.

But I would have you without carefulness. He that is unmarried careth for the things that belong to the Lord, how he may please the Lord:

But he that is married careth for the things that are of the world, how he may please his wife.

There is difference also between a wife and a virgin. The unmarried woman careth for the things of the Lord, that she may be holy both in body and in spirit: but she that is married careth for the things of the world, how she may please her husband.

And this I speak for your own profit; not that I may cast a snare upon you, but for that which is comely, and that ye may attend upon the Lord without distraction.

But if any man think that he behaveth himself uncomely toward his virgin, if she pass the flower of her age, and need so require, let him do what he will, he sinneth not: let them marry.

Nevertheless he that standeth stedfast in his heart, having no necessity, but hath power over his own will, and hath so decreed in his heart that he will keep his virgin, doeth well.

So then he that giveth her in marriage doeth well; but he that giveth her not in marriage doeth better.

The wife is bound by the law as long as her husband liveth; but if her husband be dead, she is at liberty to be married to whom she will; only in the Lord.

But she is happier if she so abide, after my judgment: and I think also that I have the Spirit of God (1 Cor. 7:25–40).

Wives, submit yourselves unto your own husbands, as it is fit in the Lord.

Husbands, love your wives, and be not bitter against them (Col. 3:18–19).

I will therefore that the younger women marry, bear children, guide the house, give none occasion to the adversary to speak reproachfully (1 Tim. 5:14).

Marriage is honourable in all, and the bed undefiled: but whoremongers and adulterers God will judge (Heb. 13:4).

Husband-Wife

Therefore shall a man leave his father and his mother, and shall cleave unto his wife: and they shall be one flesh (Gen. 2:24).

Unto the woman he said, I will greatly multiply thy sorrow and thy conception; in sorrow thou shalt bring forth children; and thy desire shall be to thy husband, and he shall rule over thee (Gen. 3:16).

When a man hath taken a new wife, he shall not go out to war, neither shall he be charged with any business: but he shall be free at home one year, and shall cheer up his wife which he hath taken (Deut. 24:5).

A virtuous woman is a crown to her husband: but she that maketh ashamed is as rottenness in his bones (Prov. 12:4).

Whoso findeth a wife findeth a good thing, and obtaineth favour of the Lord (Prov. 18:22).

It is better to dwell in a corner of the house top, than with a brawling woman in a wide house (Prov. 21:9).

Who can find a virtuous woman? for her price is far above rubies.
The heart of her husband doth safely trust in her, so that he shall have no need of spoil.
She will do him good and not evil all the days of her life.

She seeketh wool, and flax, and worketh willingly with her hands.

She is like the merchants' ships; she bringeth her food from afar.

She riseth also while it is yet night, and giveth meat to her household, and a portion to her maidens.

She considereth a field, and buyeth it: with the fruit of her hands she planteth a vineyard.

She girdeth her loins with strength, and strengtheneth her arms.

She perceiveth that her merchandise is good; her candle goeth not out by night.

She layeth her hands to the spindle, and her hands hold the distaff.

She stretcheth out her hand to the poor; yea, she reacheth forth her hands to the needy.

She is not afraid of the snow for her household: for all her household are clothed with scarlet.

She maketh herself coverings of tapestry; her clothing is silk and purple.

Her husband is known in the gates, when he sitteth among the elders of the land.

She maketh fine linen, and selleth it; and delivereth girdles unto the merchant.

Strength and honour are her clothing; and she shall rejoice in time to come.

She openeth her mouth with wisdom; and in her tongue is the law of kindness.

She looketh well to the ways of her household, and eateth not the bread of idleness.

Her children arise up, and call her blessed; her husband also, and he praiseth her.

Many daughters have done virtuously, but thou excellest them all.

Favour is deceitful, and beauty is vain: but a woman that feareth the Lord, she shall be praised.

Give her of the fruit of her hands; and let her own works praise her in the gates (Prov. 31:10–31).

The Pharisees also came unto him, tempting him, and saying unto him, Is it lawful for a man to put away his wife for every cause?

And he answered and said unto them, Have ye not read, that he which made them at the beginning made them male and female,

And said, For this cause shall a man leave father and mother, and shall cleave to his wife: and they twain shall be one flesh?

Wherefore they are no more twain, but one flesh. What therefore God hath joined together, let not man put asunder (Matt. 19:3–6).

Let the husband render unto the wife due benevolence: and likewise also the wife unto the husband.

The wife hath not power of her own body, but the husband: and likewise also the husband hath not power of his own body, but the wife.

Defraud ye not one the other, except it be with consent for a time, that ye may give yourselves to fasting and prayer; and come together again, that Satan tempt you not for your incontinency (1 Cor. 7:3–5).

But I would have you know, that the head of every man is Christ; and the head of the woman is the man; and the head of Christ is God (1 Cor. 11:3).

Submitting yourselves one to another in the fear of God.

Wives, submit yourselves unto your own husbands, as unto the Lord.

For the husband is the head of the wife, even as Christ is the head of the church: and he is the saviour of the body.

Therefore as the church is subject unto Christ, so let the wives be to their own husbands in every thing.

Husbands, love your wives, even as Christ also loved the church, and gave himself for it;

That he might sanctify and cleanse it with the washing of water by the word,

That he might present it to himself a glorious church, not having spot, or wrinkle, or any such thing; but that it should be holy and without blemish.

So ought men to love their wives as their own bodies. He that loveth his wife loveth himself.

For no man ever yet hated his own flesh; but nourisheth and cherisheth it, even as the Lord the church:

For we are members of his body, of his flesh, and of his bones.

For this cause shall a man leave his father and mother, and shall be joined unto his wife, and they two shall be one flesh.

This is a great mystery: but I speak concerning Christ and the church.

Nevertheless let every one of you in particular so love his wife even as himself; and the wife see that she reverence her husband (Eph. 5:21–33).

Wives, submit yourselves unto your own husbands, as it is fit in the Lord.

Husbands, love your wives, and be not bitter against them (Col. 3:18–19).

The aged women likewise, that they be in behaviour as becometh holiness, not false accusers, not given to much wine, teachers of good things;

That they may teach the young women to be sober, to love their husbands, to love their children,

To be discreet, chaste, keepers at home, good, obedient to their own husbands, that the word of God be not blasphemed (Titus 2:3–5).

Likewise, ye wives, be in subjection to your own husbands; that, if any obey not the word, they also may without the word be won by the conversation of the wives;

While they behold your chaste conversation coupled with fear.

Whose adorning let it not be that outward adorning of plaiting the hair, and of wearing of gold, or of putting on of apparel;

But let it be the hidden man of the heart, in that which is not corruptible, even the ornament of a meek and quiet spirit, which is in the sight of God of great price.

For after this manner in the old time the holy women also, who trusted in God, adorned themselves, being in subjection unto their own husbands:

Even as Sara obeyed Abraham, calling him lord: whose daughters ye are, as long as ye do well, and are not afraid with any amazement.

Likewise, ye husbands, dwell with them according to knowledge, giving honour unto the wife, as unto the weaker vessel, and as being heirs together of the grace of life; that your prayers be not hindered (1 Pet. 3:1–7).

Sex and Sexuality

So God created man in his own image, in the image of God created he him; male and female created he them.

And God blessed them, and God said unto them, Be fruitful, and multiply, and replenish the earth, and subdue it: and have dominion over the fish of the sea, and over the fowl of the air, and over every living thing that moveth upon the earth (Gen. 1:27–28).

Therefore shall a man leave his father and his mother, and shall cleave unto his wife: and they shall be one flesh (Gen. 2:24).

Thou shalt not commit adultery (Ex. 20:14).

And if a man entice a maid that is not betrothed, and lie with her, he shall surely endow her to be his wife (Ex. 22:16).

None of you shall approach to any that is near of kin to him, to uncover their nakedness: I am the Lord (Lev. 18:6).

And the man that committeth adultery with another man's wife, even he that committeth adultery with his neighbour's wife, the adulterer and the adulteress shall surely be put to death (Lev. 20:10).

If any man take a wife, and go in unto her, and hate her,

And give occasions of speech against her, and bring up an evil name upon her, and say, I took this woman, and when I came to her, I found her not a maid:

Then shall the father of the damsel, and her mother, take and bring forth the tokens of the damsel's virginity unto the elders of the city in the gate:

And the damsel's father shall say unto the elders, I gave my daughter unto this man to wife, and he hateth her;

And, lo, he hath given occasions of speech against her, saying, I found not thy daughter a maid; and yet these are the tokens of my daughter's virginity. And they shall spread the cloth before the elders of the city.

And the elders of that city shall take that man and chastise him;

And they shall amerce him in an hundred shekels of silver, and give them unto the father of the damsel, because he hath brought up an evil name upon a virgin of Israel: and she shall be his wife; he may not put her away all his days.

But if this thing be true, and the tokens of virginity be not found for the damsel:

Then they shall bring out the damsel to the door of her father's house, and the men of her city shall stone her with stones that she die: because she hath wrought folly in Israel, to play the whore in her father's house: so shalt thou put evil away from among you.

If a man be found lying with a woman married to an husband, then they shall both of them die, both the man that lay with the woman, and the woman: so shalt thou put away evil from Israel (Deut. 22:13–22).

Ye have heard that it was said by them of old time, Thou shalt not commit adultery:

But I say unto you, Thou whosoever looketh on a woman to lust after her hath committed adultery with her already in his heart (Matt. 5:27–28).

For out of the heart proceed evil thoughts, murders, adulteries, fornications, thefts, false witness, blasphemies:

These are the things which defile a man: but to eat with unwashen hands defileth not a man (Matt. 15:19–20).

For this cause God gave them up unto vile affections: for even their women did change the natural use into that which is against nature:

And likewise also the men, leaving the natural use of the woman, burned in their lust one toward another; men with men working that which is unseemly, and receiving in themselves that recompence of their error which was meet (Rom. 1:26–27).

Know ye not that the unrighteous shall not inherit the kingdom of God? Be not deceived: neither fornicators, nor idolaters, nor adulterers, nor effeminate, nor abusers of themselves with mankind,

Nor thieves, nor covetous, nor drunkards, nor revilers, nor extortioners, shall inherit the kingdom of God (1 Cor. 6:9–10).

Nevertheless, to avoid fornication, let every man have his own wife, and let every woman have her own husband.

Let the husband render unto the wife due benevolence: and likewise also the wife unto the husband.

The wife hath not power of her own body, but the husband: and likewise also the husband hath not power of his own body, but the wife.

Defraud ye not one the other, except it be with consent for a time, that ye may give yourselves to fasting and prayer; and come together again, that Satan tempt you not for your incontinency.

But I speak this by permission, and not of commandment (1 Cor. 7:2–6).

For this is the will of God, even your sanctification, that ye should abstain from fornication:

That every one of you should know how to possess his vessel in sanctification and honour;

Not in the lust of concupiscence, even as the Gentiles which know not God:

That no man go beyond and defraud his brother in any matter: because that the Lord is the avenger of all such, as we also have forewarned you and testified.

For God hath not called us unto uncleanness, but unto holiness.

He therefore that despiseth, despiseth not man, but God, who hath also given unto us his holy Spirit (1 Thess. 4:3–8).

Parent-Child Relations

Honour thy father and thy mother: that thy days may be long upon the land which the Lord thy God giveth thee (Ex. 20:12).

And he that curseth his father, or his mother, shall surely be put to death (Ex. 21:17).

And these words, which I command thee this day, shall be in thine heart:

And thou shalt teach them diligently unto thy children, and shalt talk of them when thou sittest in thine house, and when thou walkest by the way, and when thou liest down, and when thou risest up (Deut. 6:6–7).

If a man have a stubborn and rebellious son, which will not obey the voice of his father, or the voice of his mother, and that, when they have chastened him, will not hearken unto them:

Then shall his father and his mother lay hold on him, and bring him out unto the elders of his city, and unto the gate of his place;

And they shall say unto the elders of his city, This our son is stubborn and rebellious, he will not obey our voice; he is a glutton, and a drunkard.

And all the men of his city shall stone him with stones, that he die: so shalt thou put evil away from among you; and all Israel shall hear, and fear (Deut. 21:18–21).

Like as a father pitieth his children, so the Lord pitieth them that fear him (Ps. 103:13).

Lo, children are an heritage of the Lord: and the fruit of the womb is his reward.

As arrows are in the hand of a mighty man; so are children of the youth.

Happy is the man that hath his quiver full of them: they shall not be ashamed, but they shall speak with the enemies in the gate (Ps. 127:3–5).

My son, hear the instruction of thy father, and forsake not the law of thy mother:

For they shall be an ornament of grace unto thy head, and chains about thy neck (Prov. 1:8–9).

Hear, ye children, the instruction of a father, and attend to know understanding.

For I give you good doctrine, forsake ye not my law.

For I was my father's son, tender and only beloved in the sight of my mother.

He taught me also, and said unto me, Let thine heart retain my words: keep my commandments, and live (Prov. 4:1–4).

The proverbs of Solomon. A wise son maketh a glad father: but a foolish son is the heaviness of his mother (Prov. 10:1).

He that spareth his rod hateth his son: but he that loveth him chasteneth him betimes (Prov. 13:24).

Chasten thy son while there is hope, and let not thy soul spare for his crying (Prov. 19:18).

Train up a child in the way he should go: and when he is old, he will not depart from it (Prov. 22:6).

Hearken unto thy father that begat thee, and despise not thy mother when she is old (Prov. 23:22).

Correct thy son, and he shall give thee rest; yea, he shall give delight unto thy soul (Prov. 29:17).

When Jesus therefore saw his mother, and the disciple standing by, whom he loved, he saith unto his mother, Woman, behold thy son!
Then saith he to the disciple, Behold thy mother! And from that hour that disciple took her unto his own home (John 19:26–27).

Behold, the third time I am ready to come to you; and I will not be burdensome to you: for I seek not yours, but you: for the children ought not to lay up for the parents, but the parents for the children (2 Cor. 12:14).

Children, obey your parents in the Lord: for this is right.
Honour thy father and mother; which is the first commandment with promise;
That it may be well with thee, and thou mayest live long on the earth.
And, ye fathers, provoke not your children to wrath: but bring them up in the nurture and admonition of the Lord (Eph. 6:1–4).

Children, obey your parents in all things: for this is well pleasing unto the Lord.
Fathers, provoke not your children to anger, lest they be discouraged (Col. 3:20–21).

That they may teach the young women to be sober, to love their husbands, to love their children (Titus 2:4).

Divorce

A widow, or a divorced woman, or profane, or an harlot, these shall he not take: but he shall take a virgin of his own people to wife.

Neither shall he profane his seed among his people: for I the Lord do sanctify him (Lev. 21:14–15).

But if the priest's daughter be a widow, or divorced, and have no child, and is returned unto her father's house, as in her youth, she shall eat of her father's meat: but there shall no stranger eat thereof (Lev. 22:13).

When a man hath taken a wife, and married her, and it come to pass that she find no favour in his eyes, because he hath found some uncleanness in her: then let him write her a bill of divorcement, and give it in her hand, and send her out of his house.

And when she is departed out of his house, she may go and be another man's wife.

And if the latter husband hate her, and write her a bill of divorcement, and giveth it in her hand, and sendeth her out of his house; or if the latter husband die, which took her to be his wife;

Her former husband, which sent her away, may not take her again to be his wife, after that she is defiled; for that is abomination before the Lord: and thou shalt not cause the land to sin, which the Lord thy God giveth thee for an inheritance (Deut. 24:1–4).

And did not he make one? Yet had he the residue of the spirit. And wherefore one? That he might seek a godly seed. Therefore take heed to your spirit, and let none deal treacherously against the wife of his youth.

For the Lord, the God of Israel, saith that he hateth putting away: for one covereth violence with his garment, saith the Lord of hosts: therefore take heed to your spirit, that ye deal not treacherously (Mal. 2:15–16).

It hath been said, Whosoever shall put away his wife, let him give her a writing of divorcement:

But I say unto you, That whosoever shall put away his wife, saving for the cause of fornication, causeth her to commit adultery: and whosoever shall marry her that is divorced committeth adultery (Matt. 5:31–32).

And the Pharisees came to him, and asked him, Is it lawful for a man to put away his wife? tempting him.

And he answered and said unto them, What did Moses command you?

And they said, Moses suffered to write a bill of divorcement, and to put her away.

And Jesus answered and said unto them, For the hardness of your heart he wrote you this precept.

But from the beginning of the creation of God made them male and female.

For this cause shall a man leave his father and mother, and cleave to his wife;

And they twain shall be one flesh: so then they are no more twain, but one flesh.

What therefore God hath joined together, let not man put asunder.

And in the house his disciples asked him again of the same matter.

And he saith unto them, Whosoever shall put away his wife, and marry another, committeth adultery against her.

And if a woman shall put away her husband, and be married to another, she committeth adultery (Mark 10:2–12).

Whosoever putteth away his wife, and marrieth another, committeth adultery: and whosoever marrieth her that is put away from her husband committeth adultery (Luke 16:18).

Know ye not, brethren, (for I speak to them that know the law,) how that the law hath dominion over a man as long as he liveth?

For the woman which hath an husband is bound by the law to her husband so long as he liveth; but if the husband be dead, she is loosed from the law of her husband.

So then if, while her husband liveth, she be married to another man, she shall be called an adulteress: but if her husband be dead, she is free from that law; so that she is no adulteress, though she be married to another man (Rom. 7:1–3).

But to the rest speak I, not the Lord: If any brother hath a wife that believeth not, and she be pleased to dwell with him, let him not put her away.

And the woman which hath an husband that believeth not, and if he be pleased to dwell with her, let her not leave him.

For the unbelieving husband is sanctified by the wife, and the unbelieving wife is sanctified by the husband: else were your children unclean; but now are they holy.

But if the unbelieving depart, let him depart. A brother or a sister is not under bondage in such cases: but God hath called us to peace (1 Cor. 7:12–15).

Index of Scripture References

OLD TESTAMENT

	Page
GENESIS	
1:27	29
1:27–28	26, 153
1:28	17
2:18–24	11, 146
2:20–23	17
2:24	13, 16, 28, 149, 153
3:16	149
15:15	114
25:8	114
EXODUS	
20:12	114, 155
20:14	24, 153
21:17	155
22:16	153
LEVITICUS	
18:6	153
19:32	114
20:10	153
21:14–15	158
22:13	158
DEUTERONOMY	
4:40	114
5:33	114
6:3–12	101, 102
6:6–7	17, 102, 155
11:19–21	114
21:18–21	156
22:13–22	154

	Page
24:1–4	158
24:5	149
32:7	110, 115
JUDGES	
8:32	114
2 SAMUEL	
18:24–33	93
18:33	92
1 KINGS	
3:14	114
1 CHRONICLES	
29:28	114
JOB	
5:26	114
32:4	114
42:17	114
PSALMS	
7:9, 18	115
46:1	81
71:9, 18	115
90:10	116
91:2	64
91:5–6	58, 59
91:9–10	64
91:16	59, 114
103:13	156
127:3–5	156
PROVERBS	
1:8–9	156

	Page			Page
3:1–2	114		31:10–31	150
3:13–16	114		ECCLESIASTES	
4:1–4	156		11:8	116
9:10–11	114		12:1–7	115, 116
10:1	156		ISAIAH	
12:4	149		46:4	114
13:24	157		JEREMIAH	
18:22	146, 149		6:11	116
19:18	157		29:6	147
20:29	114		JOEL	
21:9	149		1:2–3	116
22:6	17, 157		MALACHI	
23:22	110, 114, 157		2:15–16	158
29:7	157		3:6	65

NEW TESTAMENT

	Page			Page
MATTHEW			MARK	
5	102		10:2–12	159
5:27–28	23, 154		10:14	56
5:27–30	24		10:15	55
5:31–32	159		LUKE	
7:7–11	34		2:42–52	120
11:1–6	116		4:16–21	116
14:19	127		10:25–37	115
14:27	81		16:18	159
15:1–9	114		23:46	81
15:3–6	106		JOHN	
15:19–20	154		3:14–18	115
19	102		10:10	23
19:3–6	151		14:1–4	116
19:4–6	13		14:6	100
19:6	15		14:18	81
19:8	15		19:26–27	157
19:15	15		20:21	127
22:23–30	147		21:17	66
22:34–40	115		21:18–22	66
25:31–46	116		ACTS	
27:46	75, 81		1:8	128

Page

ROMANS

1:26–27   154
7:1–3   147, 159
8:28   115
8:31–39   82
8:37   82

1 CORINTHIANS

6:9–10   154
7   17, 102
7:1–5   15, 27
7:2   15
7:2–6   17, 155
7:3–5   151
7:8–9   147
7:12–15   160
7:25–40   148
11:3   151
13   19

2 CORINTHIANS

8:7–15   107
12:14   107, 157

EPHESIANS

4:26   79
5–6   102
5:21–33   19, 152
6:1–4   19, 157
6:2   114
6:4   17

COLOSSIANS

1:24   116
3   102
3:18–19   149, 152

Page

3:20–21   157
4:15   20

1 THESSALONIANS

4:3–8   155

1 TIMOTHY

5:1–2   114
5:3–16   107
5:4, 8   114
5:8   17, 106, 114
5:11–13   85
5:14   149

2 TIMOTHY

1:5   17, 83, 88, 107
1:7   115
3:6–7   83, 85

TITUS

2:3–4   83
2:3–5   19, 85, 152
2:4   158

HEBREWS

13:4   17, 27, 149

1 PETER

3:1–2, 7   19
3:1–7   152
4:12–19   116

1 JOHN

1:9   81
2:12–14   48
2:13   55
3:14–18   115

REVELATION

21:4   116

Subject Index

Adoption, 85
Adultery, 15–16, 23–33, 59, 92, 145
Aging, 58, 60, 66–74, 106, 110–119, 131, 133–134, 136
Aging, preparation for, 66–74, 117
Aging, problems of, 68, 111–114
Aging, challenges of, 111, 115–116
Adolescent (see Youth)
Anger, 37–38, 77, 79
Anxiety, 77, 79–80, 123
Authority, 64

Behavior, 70, 96
Bestiality, 24
Bible, 17, 19–20, 32, 57, 81–82, 87, 102–104, 116, 126, 129, 132, 139, 143, 145–146
Birth, 12, 17, 34, 84–85
Birth Control, 136
Birthdays, 22
Busyness, 59–60, 64, 106, 121, 125

Character, 53, 70, 94
Change, 59–60
Childhood, 34–49
Childless Couple, 135
Children, 17, 21, 30, 34, 47, 83–100, 103, 131–133, 135–136
Church, 15, 20–21, 51–53, 73, 77, 82, 87–88, 104–105, 108–109, 114–119, 124–126, 130–144
Comfort, 72–73, 81–82, 127
Controversy, 140–141

Conversion, 86–88
Convictions, 96
Communication, 18, 64, 130, 135–137
Courtesy, 19–20

Deacons, 51–52
Death, 71–73, 76–80, 83–84, 113–114, 119, 122–123
Decision making, 39–40, 65
Delinquency, 59, 94–95, 145
Depression, 77, 112, 123
Devotionals (see Worship, family)
Discipleship, 101–109
Discipline, 17, 19, 40–42, 46, 95–97
Divorce, 15, 59, 76–80, 107, 122–123, 131, 135, 137

Education, 117, 121–122, 133–134
Empty Nest, 64, 134
Engagement, 14, 134
Enrichment, 139
Evangelism, 20, 107–109, 116–117, 127–128, 139, 143
Exclusiveness, 15–17

Faith, 22, 33, 56–57, 65, 70, 86, 88, 100, 116, 128
Family (see Marriage)
Family Cycle, 58–59, 69
Failure, 15, 77–78, 89–100, 137
Father, 16, 48, 52, 54
Fatherhood, 92–100

Fears, 60–61, 65, 68, 71, 79–80, 95, 112, 115–116
Fidelity, 19, 25, 30
Finances, 61–62, 112–113, 122
Forgiveness, 32–33, 55, 78, 81, 90–91, 99–100
Fornication, 24
Friendship, 73, 76, 80, 113, 124
Frustration, 61, 65
Fun (see Play)
Future, 66–74

Giving, 70
God, 21–22, 23–33, 45–47, 55–57, 63–65, 67–68, 70–74, 76, 78–79, 81–82, 84, 86, 88–92, 98–100, 105, 109, 115, 123, 129
Grace, 55, 91
Greed, 27
Grief, 77, 98–100, 127
Grandparents, 83–84, 95, 110, 122
Growth, physical, 48–57
Growth, spiritual, 32–33, 48–57, 74, 102–105
Guilt, 26, 32–33, 77–78, 89–90, 142

Happiness, 62, 74, 129
Heaven, 73, 86
Hell, 73
Health, 27, 69–71, 79, 112, 117–119, 122
Holidays, 43, 106, 122–128, 138
Holy Spirit, 22, 32, 45, 69
Homosexuality, 25
Honeymoon, 16, 134
Honor, 19
Hope, 82, 100, 111
Housing, 112–113, 117, 131, 134
Husband-Wife, 18–19, 44, 58–60, 62–64, 75, 85, 134–136, 144–145

Incest, 24, 92, 145
Illness, 114–116

Infant, 84–86
In-laws, 113, 134–136

Joy, 65, 128
Jesus Christ, 15, 22, 33, 40, 45–47, 57, 65–68, 70–74, 76, 81–82, 86, 88, 100–102, 123–128

Leisure (see Play, Recreation)
Life, 48–57, 58–65, 66–74, 116
Loneliness, 68, 72–73, 77, 80 112, 127
Love, 12, 14, 19–20, 31–33, 34–38, 45, 70, 76–78, 82, 88, 97
Love, importance of, 35, 97
Love, inadequacy of, 14–15
Love, ways to express, 36–38, 95–97, 107
Loyalty, 17–33

Marriage, 13, 134–136
Marriage, attitude toward, 12
Marriage, a union, 12, 13–16, 28–30
Marriage, myths about, 12
Marriage, nature of, 13
Marriage, purpose of, 17–19, 29
Marriage, threats to, 13, 16, 29, 58–65
Marriage, trial, 12
Materialism, 27, 61–62, 97, 126–127
Meals, 18, 112, 118
Middle adults, 48–57, 58–65
Ministry, 15, 20, 51–52, 68, 70, 73, 106–107, 116–119, 130–134
Mistakes, 88–89
Money (see Finances)
Mother, 16, 83–84
Motherhood, 83–91

Nagging, 20, 96
Neglect, 97–98

Obedience, 19, 64, 115
Orderliness, 42–46

Pain, 72–82
Parent-Child, 19–20, 34–47, 53–55,
  61, 63–64, 83–91, 92–100, 106,
  114, 136, 145
Parents, 16, 34–47, 50–53, 94, 96–
  97, 103, 134–135
Peace, 64
Personality, 94–95
Play, 19, 43, 54
Pleasure, 29
Pornography, 25
Poverty, 131–133, 135
Prayer, 17, 19, 21, 32, 43, 109, 117,
  126
Preaching, 129–130, 134, 137–144
Preoccupation, 62–63
Pride, 27, 62
Procreation, 17, 29–30
Purpose, 63, 65, 111

Recreation, 131–132
Rejection, 31, 75, 77–82
Relationships, 14, 19–20, 76, 79–
  80, 82
Respect, 19, 114, 117, 124
Responsibility, 17, 25, 30, 85, 90–
  91, 94, 98, 115
Retirement, 56, 113, 115, 134
Revival, 108
Routine, 58, 61, 121–122
Repentance, 22, 32–33, 99–100
Rituals, 43

Satan, 56
Salvation, 55, 72, 86
Security, 43–44, 46
Self-image, 38–39
Selfishness, 31, 59, 70
Senior Adults, 48–57, 110–119

Separation, 62, 76–78
Sex, 12, 15, 23–33, 60–61, 63, 69,
  81, 132
Sharing, 18
Sin, 31, 55, 78, 81, 88–90, 99
Single Adults, 75–82, 135
Single Parents, 81, 135
Skills, 40, 55, 86, 88
Social Concerns, 106–107, 121
Spiritual Growth (see Growth,
  spiritual)
Supervision, 17, 38–40, 45
Suspicion, 80

Time, 18, 52, 97–98
Togetherness, 16, 18–19, 43–44,
  46, 64
Traditions, 43
Travel, 113, 118–120, 122
Trust, 64–65, 67, 73, 80, 115

Union, 13–16, 29
Unwed mothers, 39

Values, 65

Weddings, 16, 134
Widow, 106, 107
Wife-Husband, 18–19, 44, 58–60,
  62–64, 75, 85, 134–135, 144–145
Will of God, 12, 14–15, 17, 24, 35,
  46, 65, 71
Work, 19
Worship, 46, 89, 105–106, 124
Worship, church, 21–22, 46, 105–
  106, 126
Worship, family, 20–22, 44–45, 89,
  105–106

Youth, 48–57, 67, 96–97
Young Adults, 48, 58–59